# A DUEL OF BULLS

## HEMINGWAY AND WELLES IN LOVE AND WAR

### PETE CARVILL

\B<sup>b</sup>\

Biteback Publishing

First published in Great Britain in 2025 by
Biteback Publishing Ltd, London
Copyright © Pete Carvill 2025

Pete Carvill has asserted his right under the Copyright, Designs and Patents Act 1988 to be
identified as the author of this work.

ISBN 978-1-78590-896-5

10 9 8 7 6 5 4 3 2 1

A CIP catalogue record for this book is available from the British Library.

Set in Minion Pro and CoFo Kabeltouw

Printed and bound in Great Britain by
CPI Group (UK) Ltd, Croydon CR0 4YY

FSC
www.fsc.org
MIX
Paper | Supporting
responsible forestry
FSC® C013604

*For Laurence and Kevin.*

*Some of us fell along the way. This book is dedicated to two of them.*

*Pete.*

*'Ladies and gentlemen, by way of introduction, this is a film about trickery and fraud. About lies. Tell it by the fireside or in a marketplace or in a movie. Almost any story is almost certainly some kind of lie.'*
– ORSON WELLES, *F FOR FAKE*


*'I'd say you were doing something pretty dangerous this time. Mixing fact and fiction.'*
– MR POPESCU, *THE THIRD MAN*

# CONTENTS

## ACT THREE: ONE BULL AT SUNDOWN (1961 TO 1985)

# INTRODUCTION

# STORYTELLING (2025)

*'Existence, the physical universe, is basically playful.'*
– ALAN WATTS

**W**riting is easier than any other profession. You sit and write or type, and eventually you wind up with something that you then have to cut down, edit, rewrite or simply dump. There are always fears about getting the facts and, most importantly, the words right.

But it is not a hard job, certainly nowhere near as tiresome as mining or nursing. There is no great muscle strain, dealing with the general public or – until the final stages at least, when an editor gets involved – any kind of boss.

Fears, however, remain, as well as challenges.

There have been challenges in producing this book; to write *A Duel of Bulls: Hemingway and Welles in Love and War* is to write about the two, at times intertwined, lives of two men renowned for their capacity to embellish, lie and – frequently – bullshit.

Parsing fact from fiction is hard here and impossible there. And there are missed connections, inferences either ignored or paid

too-close attention and missing facts. Lives lived so fully that they cannot be contained within a single book.

That is why this is not a serious academic work on either Ernest Hemingway or Orson Welles. There are as many facts included as possible, along with some creative licence taken in places to string them together. But *A Duel of Bulls* is primarily a form of entertainment. A piece of fun. Something to take you from one moment into the next.

There will be, by necessity, errors and omissions, both purposeful and accidental. And, as both men were unreliable narrators of their own lives, it would be churlish not to continue that tradition in these pages.

The academics will find holes and cavities in this work. They will say that this thing or that thing is missing, that a certain person or event or turning point has not been accounted for or has been miscalculated in its importance. That a certain event or conversation did not happen *that* way, if it happened at all. But the academics can have their books; this one is mine. Besides, there is always some fool who turns up and ruins the fun for everyone by knowing the correct answer.

And with that, our story begins...

# 'HE WAS A VERY CLOSE FRIEND OF MINE' (1973)

It was the end of the year and he was back, in London, on another chat show. It had been twelve years since Ernest Hemingway's death, and it was only another twelve before his own. Orson Welles had reached the time of his life when he would talk more about what he had done rather than what he was going to do.

He was as large as he ever would be, and he sat deeply in the black leather chair, his stomach out halfway to his knees. He was dressed in black trousers and a black shirt, with an olive-green light jacket. His hair and beard were mostly grey. He was fifty-eight years old and still struggling, despite everything, despite of or maybe *because* of his reputation, to make his films. There was this project and that project, another project here and another one there, all of them calling for his attention, all of them needing money. So he went from country to country, from sofa to dressing room to film sets that were not his to potential investors, and he tried to drum up interest at each. Just a few more dollars, a bit more funding, and he would be able to finish something, finish *anything*.

He had already told the host to put aside his questions. The best

thing to do, he said, was just to talk. Besides, he was practised at that, able to recite and retell his stories easily. And he had always been a performer, so it was easy to entertain this crowd. Or any crowd.

He picked up his walking stick. 'Well, I don't think I'm going to sparkle tonight, Michael,' he said to the host, a practised glint in his eye, 'but I have my stick and if you try one of those in-depth interviews, you ought to know that I'm armed!'

They spoke for ten minutes or so before the subject of bullfighting came up.

'Are you, in fact,' asked the host, 'also still interested – and I know it was a passion of yours in previous years – in bullfighting?'

'Yes,' said Welles, 'but less – I'm interested in what I remember. I don't like it much any more.'

'Why is that?'

Welles lit his cigar and put it in his mouth. He inhaled. 'Well, two things.' He took the cigar out of his mouth. 'First of all, bullfighting, as somebody once said very well, is indefensible and irresistible. And it is irresistible when everything is as it ought to be, both with the beast – the sacrificial beast – and with the brave man who meets that brave animal for a ritualistic encounter.'

Welles reflected on the bullfights. He shook his hand above his head, a wave that turned into him smoothing down his hair.

'I'm not going to go into all that mystique,' he said, 'which has been pretty worn out. But now the fact is that it has become an industry which depends on, for its existence, the tourist trade, so it's become folkloric. And I hate anything which is folkloric, you know. But I haven't turned against bullfighting because it needs a lot of Japanese in the front row to keep it going, and it does. I've turned against it for very much the same reason that my father, who

was a great hunter, suddenly stopped hunting. He said, "I've killed enough animals, and I'm ashamed of myself."'

Welles thought about the hundreds, thousands, of bullfights that he had seen and of what he had learned from them. He thought the time had been wasted. He said he had seen enough of the animals die.

'Wasn't I living second-hand through the lives of those *toreros* who were my friends?' he reflected. 'Wasn't I living and dying second-hand? Wasn't there something finally voyeuristic about it? I suspect my *afición*.'

His voice changed. An admission. 'I still go to bullfights,' he said, almost with a shrug. 'I'm not totally reformed.'

The host pushed a little more on bullfighting. There was another famous American afficionado of it, he said. Ernest Hemingway.

'Did you ever meet him?' the host asked.

'He was a very close friend of mine,' said Welles. 'I knew him on and off for many years. We had a very strange relationship.'

The line sounded practised, the default defence to the question. But there were notes of truth. And there was certainly more there, maybe more so than even Welles could articulate.

ACT ONE

# TWO BULLS AT DAWN (1929 TO 1937)

# 1

# THE MOST CELEBRATED WRITER IN AMERICA IS BORED (1929 TO 1932)

**I**t was 1929 and Ernest Hemingway was living in Key West, Florida, where he liked to rise early in the morning when the air was still cool, go to his desk and write 500 words.

It would become too hot after that, with the dense and humid air seeming to invade everything. The noises would come, too, with people toing and froing in the streets, their conversations being carried along on the air and into the office he used. It was then that he would take himself off to play with Patrick, his second son and the first of the two boys he would have with Pauline, Wife #2, for a few hours.

He could be found later on most days in the bar of Sloppy Joe's, over on Duval Street. He liked it there. They did not care in that place about what he wore. It was a thing that they had in common, as he did not care about what he wore, either. Pauline would always chide him for wearing this shirt or that shirt or for not having a tie. But he was comfortable in those old and dirty shorts, cinched together with a knotted rope. And the people down there, in the south of Florida, already knew him so well that changing his look

at this point… Well, that would be something false, wouldn't it? A piece of his life without the ring of truth to it that he tried to live by.

At the end of each week, he would go to the fights, where they would sometimes let him referee. But if he was not in the ring, he would sit and drink beer that had been stored in large chests of cold water and ice. And he was happy there, too, on those evenings when he could just sit on the low wooden benches with the heat hanging in the air and flecks of cold water dotting his hands, wrists and arms. But if he did get up, he would sometimes hear the voices say as he climbed up those three steps and went between the ropes, 'Hey, that's Ernest Hemingway, the writer. He lives around here.'

Those words were always said with a whisper, like a secret thrown quickly between friends. But he liked the recognition. He liked people to know who he was, even if he insisted that everyone treat him like anybody else.

It seemed to be a good life, but he felt like a man with an itch in his lower back that he was unable to scratch. Uncomfortable, most of the time.

His wife Pauline was dedicated to him, and that was good in its own way. And his books were selling. And the people and the critics liked those books. And he was treated like someone whose views were worth listening to. And that was good, too.

The thing with Pauline's uncle Gus was one that he did not like, but he did not say anything. The house was Gus's and so was the money that maintained it. And then there was Pauline's trust fund, and it was that and Gus's money that paid for the trips and the lifestyle. He loved all those things, and it was those things – the freedom to do anything he wanted, paid for by that money – that made him more than just a writer.

He would admit that it was a good life. He could admit that. Even

if the life was not yet entirely his, like a suit and a mask that he was pulling on slowly. *The only way to guarantee success*, he thought, *was to be successful.*

Sometimes, Florida scared him. The heat and the family made him feel blocked. He feared becoming stagnant. He needed something new. He was a fiction writer, and the critics and the public loved him for that. He had done *The Sun Also Rises*. That was the big one. Then *Men Without Women*. Then there was *A Farewell to Arms*. Everything he wrote was moulded from the clay of his own life. He had mined those early trips to Spain with Hadley, Wife #1, for the first book, then that time with the nurse in Italy for *Farewell*.

That taking of his own life and moulding it was something that he had to do. He was no good at plots; they were not something for an old newspaper man. He could deal in facts and stories but not in the whimsical twists and turns it took to falsely snare a reader.

The public knew it. His publishers knew it. And because he wrote from his own life, he thought that he would write now about life properly. And death.

He had loved Spain almost from the start. That had been with Stein – his writer friend, his mentor. She was the one who had got him into the bullfights with her talk and her pictures of the *torero* Joselito. That was in 1923.

'You should see it, Ernest,' she had told him one afternoon in Paris. 'It's all there.'

'It's all there?'

'Life and death. Is there anything else?'

'What about the poor horses?'

'They are indeed poor. But there is also Joselito. And if you cannot

get to him – and you will, because I will introduce you – there is his brother Gallo.'

'I want to write about life and death,' he told her.

'Then you need to go to Spain. It is the only place where you can see *violent* death now that all the wars are long over.'

'I very much want to go.'

'Are you sure?'

'Yes. I'm trying to learn to write, starting with the simplest things. And one of the simplest things of all, and the most fundamental, is violent death.'

He travelled to Spain with friends that summer in 1923. It was his first time. They spent a month there, starting in Madrid and then moving around: Seville, Ronda, Grenada, Toledo. They saw every bullfight that they could. Then he went back to Paris and to Hadley, and he brought her down with him to Pamplona. They became *aficionados* of the bullfights.

He wrote later in a letter to his former Chicago roommate: 'Spain is damn good in hot weather.'

Lower down on the page, he wrote:

You'd be crazy about a really good bullfight, Bill. It isn't just brutal like they always told us. It's a great tragedy – and the most beautiful thing I've ever seen and takes more guts and skills and guts again than anything possibly could. It's just like having a ringside seat at the war with nothing going to happen to you.

He managed to persuade his newspaper, the *Toronto Star*, to pay him for two articles on the subject in 1923. 'Bullfighting is not a

sport,' he wrote piously. 'It was never meant to be. It is a tragedy. A very great tragedy. The tragedy is the death of the bull.' It was less a guide to the fights and the festivals that he wrote but more a guide to himself, an advert of the life he was living. He wrote of Pamplona and said that it was where he had seen the best fights.

He wrote about bullfighting again the next year, in 1924, in *In Our Time*. These were small and brief pieces, a bundled-together collection of short stories, almost dashed off. But Spain held to him.

Maxwell Perkins became his editor in 1925, and the first thing Hemingway did was write him a letter about bullfighting.

'I hope some day,' wrote Hemingway,

to have a sort of Doughty's *Arabia Deserta* of the Bull Ring, a very big book with some wonderful pictures. But one has to save all winter to be able to bum in Spain in the summer and writing classics, I've always heard, takes some time. Somehow, I don't care about writing a novel and I like to write short stories and I like to work at the bullfight book so I guess I'm a bad prospect for a publisher anyway.

He and Hadley kept going back. They took more friends with them in 1925. Everyone fought on that trip, but it was good material.

He came home and wrote *The Sun Also Rises*. He based it on the friends. He based it on the good material. But when he and Hadley went to Pamplona in 1926, Pauline was there and that meant that his first marriage was ending.

Hadley gave him a divorce in 1927, and he married Pauline a few days later. Then they went to Florida, and he wrote books and articles, but he carried on thinking about Spain and the bulls. There

was a book there, he felt, and he wanted people to understand about the bullfights, to know that they were not as cruel or brutal as they seemed to be. And he wanted it for himself, to be the great American voice on bulls and men.

Pauline went with him to Spain. He wanted to go. She wanted to be with him. They visited just after they married.

He went back to America and wrote *A Farewell to Arms*. It made him think of the nurse in Italy. He wanted to think of other things.

His father died a few months later. Dr Clarence Hemingway had put a gun in his mouth. A note was struck.

Ernest Hemingway needed to think again about something else.

He decided to go back to Spain and write of the bulls and the men who fought them.

It was September 1929 and Hemingway had been following the bulls around Spain for weeks. Now, he was looking for the Cafe Gran Via in the centre of Madrid. There was one *torero* that he was keen to meet.

The day was hot, and he was sweating in the heat of the late afternoon. It was thicker and fuller than in Florida, and it settled and moistened his armpits and the backs of his legs. The skin of his bad knee squeaked against the rubber brace that kept it in place.

He saw the cafe then, and his eyes settled on the party sat outside. He scanned the crowd for a face familiar from newsprint: the Jewish bullfighter from New York, the one that the papers wrote all the stories about.

'Sidney Franklin?'

A small, lithe man with short red hair and pale skin looked over to him. 'I am he,' he said. He nodded.

'I believe my friend wrote to you about me.'

Franklin looked at the sweaty, dishevelled heavyset man in front

of him. Hemingway's clothes were wrinkled. There were flashes of grey in the dark stubble blanketing his chin. 'He did?'

'Yes. Guy Hickok from the *Brooklyn Eagle*. He said he would write to you about me.'

Franklin shook his head. 'No,' he said. 'But please sit down and have a drink. Where are you from?'

Hemingway took an empty seat opposite Franklin. 'Oak Park, near Chicago. But I live in Florida now.'

'I'm from Brooklyn. Your name?'

'Ernest Hemingway.'

There was a murmur behind Franklin. Some heads turned in the direction of Hemingway.

'I've heard your name.'

'Hickok wrote to you, then?'

'No, but I know your name.'

'Maybe you have read some of my stories or one of my books?'

Franklin waved dismissively. 'I'm afraid I'm not much of a reader. Are you a writer?'

Hemingway laughed. 'Yes but probably not much of one.'

'Would you like a drink? You can order anything you want.'

'Thank you, but that wouldn't be right. I'll get this.'

A waiter came over. Hemingway asked for a bottle of Pernod.

They began to talk beyond pleasantries.

'Tell me, Ernest,' said Franklin. 'I hope you don't mind me calling you "Ernest"?'

'Others call me "Papa".'

Franklin nodded. 'OK, Papa. What are you writing now?'

'Not much. I have a new book coming out in a few months. I'm calling it *A Farewell to Arms*. After that, I'm going to write something about this. Maybe about you.'

9

'About me?'

'About the bullfight.'

'And what is so interesting about the bullfight?'

'Everything.'

'That is a good answer.' Franklin reached over and took Hemingway's bottle of Pernod and poured an inch of it into his dirty wine glass. 'Do you know what I'm not going to do, Papa?' he asked, finishing the cloudy liquid in one gulp.

'No.'

'I'm not going to go back to my hometown of Brooklyn until I am famous across the whole of Spain. And I'm going to make America fall in love with the bulls. I think they just might, like they have fallen in love with all kinds of sports.'

'That is my ambition, too. It begins in Spain.'

He and Pauline went back up to Paris afterwards to see the old friends who still spoke with him after their affair and his divorce from Hadley. He asked those people not to tell F. Scott Fitzgerald where he and Pauline were.

He and Fitzgerald had a strange relationship. The younger Hemingway had often turned to the older, more erudite Fitzgerald for guidance. It was Fitzgerald who had suggested that Hemingway remove the first eight pages of *The Sun Also Rises*. Hemingway did.

But then Hemingway had become successful, and he had written three books while Fitzgerald had become a drunk. He embarrassed Hemingway, and he grasped onto their friendship with greased, stubby fingers. Hemingway had loved him. Fitzgerald had loved him, too.

Hemingway went to see Stein, and she compared him and Fitzgerald.

'The thing is, Ernest,' she said, 'that you both have flames. That is

your talent. Scott's flame shines brighter than yours, but he is going to burn out quicker than you. You will go longer.'

Hemingway thought she meant that Fitzgerald was better. Fitzgerald apologised for Stein's comments. He hoped that Hemingway would still love him.

He began writing *Death in the Afternoon* in March 1930. He had lived with the bullfights and with Spain in his head for years.

Uncle Gus helped him out again. He wrote to friends in Spain and asked them to send books and magazines to his nephew-in-law, and then uncle Gus thought again and sent a telegram so that they would get the message quicker.

Hemingway sank into the books when they came. He read. He took notes. He wrote paragraphs here and there. He thought about Franklin and included him.

In July, he and Pauline were back from Spain, and they took a road trip to Wyoming, driving from town to town, looking for a cool and quiet spot for him to write.

They ended up in Montana, and he wrote his 500 words in the morning, and then he would hunt and fish in the afternoon. Pauline read what he wrote, offered suggestions. Hemingway did not use anything that she did not like.

He picked up more injuries. They added to the concussions in Italy and in France – one in war, the other in peace. An injured knee led to septicaemia. He cut his face open when a horse he was riding on bolted through trees. The stitches gave him a permanent scowl.

In November, he was driving through the night outside Park City, Montana. It was he and the writer John Dos Passos and their friend Floyd Allington riding through the night, drunk. The road

was bad. Some headlights blitzed him, and he jerked the car up onto the side of the road and over it and into a ditch. It rolled. He broke his arm.

He spent one night on a shared ward in the hospital and, when the staff learned who he was, they moved him to a private room. The break in his arm started above the elbow and curled its way up, severe enough that the doctors needed to operate to reset it.

Hemingway was miserable. It was his right arm, and he could not work. The nerves may have been dead. He may not, physically, have been able to write again.

Pauline came to him and offered to take notes. He waved her away. 'I'm a writer,' he said. 'I have to be able to write!'

The bullfighting book moved out of his grasp. He could still see it like a mirage on the horizon. He knew the route from here to there. It moved further away.

He stayed in bed for two months. His hair and his beard grew long. His arm stayed in a splint for the longest time. He hated being immobilised. He believed that his body should not betray him. He hated the pain. He thought that if pain was to have any meaning, then it had to end. But the pain did not end.

His mood blackened. He cancelled a planned safari trip to Africa. Uncle Gus had been paying for that, too.

He went back to Key West with the arm still useless. It began to heal weeks later. Shimmers of feeling ran along his fingers and up through his arm. Long-dormant muscles began to reawaken.

One day, Pauline's mother went to see him.

'How are you, Ernest?' she asked. She would never call him 'Papa'.

He shook his head, looked into her eyes. 'The only car I want from now on,' he said, 'is one that is guaranteed to *kill* the driver!'

Pauline stepped over to them. She put her hand on her mother's arm. 'It's OK,' she said. 'Papa is OK.'

Living with him was uneasy for five months. He thought of Spain and of fishing. He thought of all the things that he could not do with this arm healing only gradually.

He would snap. His mood would blacken. He needed to write.

Spain moved further away.

The following year, 1931, began with Pauline pregnant again. He wanted a girl. He did not know what was coming.

The arm healed. He began to write again. He fiddled with short things to reopen the gates. The mind began to dredge up words, phrases, structures. He got them down on paper.

They bought a house. It was theirs.

Key West had been poor but was now becoming rich. The money flowed in. Hemingway liked to believe, even if it were not true, that he had been poor once, starving in a cold apartment in Paris.

He and Pauline sailed separately back to Europe. She went to Paris. He settled in Madrid and watched bullfights. The monarchists clashed with the police. People died.

A Spanish painter named Luis Quintanilla told him that there needed to be a revolution in Spain.

'It's a necessity,' he said. 'A forest needs an occasional fire so that it does not choke itself.'

Hemingway dipped between Spain and France, travelling around the first and then popping up to see Pauline, pregnant, in Paris. He saw Sidney Franklin again in Madrid.

In July 1931, Hemingway took his first son, Jack, with him to Pamplona. The boy lived now mostly with his mother in Chicago and

saw his father only once or twice a year. The boy reminded his father of earlier, happier, simpler times.

Hemingway had given him the middle name of 'Nicanor' after a bullfighter. That bullfighter fought that day.

Little Jack, eight years old, sat bored on the rounded stone seats of the Plaza de Toros in Pamplona. He watched one of the people he had been named after stride across the hot sand, plant his legs and kill a bull. He saw the misty spray of blood in the air, and he heard the murmuring and breaths of approval from the crowd. He hated it.

Afterward, the bullfighter Cayetano Ordóñez performed poorly. Ordóñez had been the inspiration for Pedro Romero in *The Sun Also Rises*. Hemingway hated him.

The crowd did, too. Boos ran around the arena like the sails of a ship going up. There was a single one at first, thrown down into the ring, where it landed with a thump on the dense sand, but tens, then hundreds of people were throwing their heavy, brown, leather seat cushions into the ring.

Jack tugged at his father's sleeve. Hemingway's face was tight. 'Can I throw mine, too, Papa?' Jack asked.

'If you must.'

Jack stood and picked up his cushion in both arms, then squeezed through the people and stepped down to the fence that separated the ring from the spectators. He pushed the cushion up onto its top, then pushed between the metal rails so it fell straight down into the *callejón*, a great distance from Ordóñez. He went back and sat next to his father.

Hemingway looked ahead. He shifted and twitched, the muscles in his jaw straining like hawsers.

'Why do you hate him, Papa?'

Hemingway looked down at his son. 'Cowardice,' he said, immediately. The answer was lurking just beneath the surface. It rose and bobbed upon the water. 'Cowardice, son. If you see *him*—' he jabbed his finger in the direction of Ordóñez '—if you see him, then you have before you the worst sort of cowardice.'

He kept on writing the book. He added. He pruned. He took photographs and then developed them. He asked Sidney Franklin for his knowledge, and he added that, too, to the pages. He left Pauline, pregnant, in Paris, then went to Madrid to write some more.

They went home to the States in the September after months of being in Europe. They went to Kansas City and rented an apartment.

Gregory Hemingway came into the world on 12 November 1931. His father had wanted a daughter. He did not know what was coming.

Pauline suffered, nearly died. The surgeon had to reopen the wounds and scars from Patrick three years earlier before he pulled Gregory from his mother.

Afterwards, the surgeon went out into the waiting room and saw Hemingway. 'It's another boy,' he said.

'Another boy?'

'Yes. Congratulations.'

Hemingway had wanted to call her 'Pilar'. 'Another boy?'

'Congratulations. But your wife – she will not be able to do this again.'

'Another boy.'

Pauline stayed in the hospital for a month. Hemingway went home to work on *Death in the Afternoon*.

He worked on the text into 1932. Dos Passos came to visit him in Key West and told him to cut things.

The book was finished by the middle of January. They took Greg and baptised him.

That night, Hemingway called Dos Passos.

'Dos, it's me.'

'Hem?'

'Yeah.' His voice was slurred and soft, like a drunk lover whispering on their way to bed. 'It's finished.'

'Are you drunk, Hem?'

'Call me "Papa".'

'*Papa*, are you drunk?'

'A little. But it's finished.'

'What is?'

'The book. The book is finished.' The line went silent.

Dos Passos waited. He heard a gulp, then the rustle of the handset being covered with a hand. Silence. The rustle again. 'Hem?'

'Papa.'

'*Papa*.'

'I cut out all the stuff you hated.' Another pause. 'Damn you, because they were good things to go. I think the book is best now. It's done, and the boy has been christened. And I am a little drunk.'

'You are a big drunk.'

Hemingway laughed. 'That's Dos,' he said, without explanation, and then hung up the phone.


He fought with the publisher over the photographs. He wanted 100. They offered him sixteen pictures. He fought. They offered him thirty-two. He fought. They let him have sixty-four.

He accepted, then went to Havana to fish for two months.

He slipped into black moods that he tried to lift by writing short stories, small sips of that needed medicine. He waited.

The book came out in September. Some reviewers loved it. Some were indifferent. He preferred the ones who loved it. He slapped across the face one who did not.

# 2

# EL AMERICANO (1933)

**O**rson Welles woke in his room on the fourth floor of a compact building in Seville. It was late, and he – just a few weeks past his eighteenth birthday – rolled over once again in the bed, pulled the thin sheet back above his slender shoulders and tried once more to sleep. He lay on his side for a few more moments and, despite promising to himself that he would not open his eyes, did so.

'Damn it,' he said.

He rolled over onto his back and looked up at the tan ceiling above his head. Then he looked around the room and his brain began to fire into motion with each image that passed into his eyes, his pulse like the hum of a movie camera.

'Damn it,' he said, again, to the empty room.

He turned a few degrees to his right and sighted the half-empty bottle of water on the stool beside the bed, its glass all scuffed. He pushed himself up onto one elbow and drank from it. The water was expectedly warm and had that metallic, coppery smell that came with the water in Seville.

He looked down at his naked feet and the toes that were nearly

touching the end of the single bed. He tapped the big one of his right foot against the bed's dark and wooden frame.

'I'm still here,' he said. 'Still here.'

He lay back and closed his eyes once more, but he knew that sleep was not going to return. He exhaled for as long as he could, and he let the warm and dry air empty from his chest. Then he opened his eyes and looked once more at the ceiling.

'Better get up.'

He sat up and then turned, putting his feet on the floor. The tiles, which he had noted grimly and morosely when taking the room a week ago, were the colour of dried blood and as cool beneath his soles as running water.

He breathed once more, and he took in the room that would house him for another three weeks. He tried to drink another mouthful of water but thought better of it and spat it back into the bottle.

It was a small room that kept easily a small single bed but not much more, an after-thought tacked onto the hotel for single, poor travellers. It had in its corner a small wardrobe, next to which he had placed his two empty cases, a tall iron stand with a mirror and basin and an old wooden desk on which he had placed the rented Corona typewriter.

*I should write today*, he thought glumly. *But only after breakfast.*

He got up and walked to the room's door, where he listened for the sounds of voices or footsteps in the corridor. He pressed his ear to the wood and listened while holding his breath.

There was no one there.

Quickly, for he had slept naked, he unlocked the door, cracked it open an inch and looked down the corridor. There was no one there, so he opened it a few more inches, reached down and picked

up the porcelain pitcher of cold water that the hotel manager had left.

After locking the door, he went back in and poured half of the pitcher into the basin, lowered his head to the water and splashed himself across the face and beneath his arms. Flecks of cold water collected in drops upon his ears.

Welles leaned forwards until his face was less than the distance of a finger length away from the mirror. He shook his chin, stretching out the line of his jaw and then he turned his head from one side to the other, trying to see himself from three different angles.

He pursed up his top lip and looked at his teeth. He did not know why. Then he rubbed at the light stubble on his chin and above his mouth and resolved that he would get a shave once he had some money.

Then there was the nose. This was the part he did not like. It was too pugnacious, too short. It was like there was this great expanse of his face, upon which he could register so much, which then bunched up so tightly into this small, button-like nose. He would always believe that his visage had taken on the shape and dimensions of an onion laid on its side, its stalk moving into the world always a half inch in front of him.

Welles took a step back from the mirror and raised his arms. He brought them together and made a quick buzzing noise like a wasp.

'*Hazzap!*' he barked, under his breath. 'Just like magic.'

But the nose was still there.

'Oh well,' he said.

He dressed quickly into a pair of dark trousers and a white shirt, then left the room, locking the door behind him. He passed other rooms, from which he heard faint and light snores. He stopped and

took a copy of the *International Herald Tribune* that his neighbour had ordered but not woken early enough to prevent its theft. He folded the paper over and slipped it behind him, into the waistband of his trousers.

He stepped out of the hotel corridor and went down to the second floor. Before he turned and went down the next flight of stairs, he stopped and looked at the locked wooden door on the landing, the one that led into the rooms of whiskey and girls that he was doing his best to avoid. There was an extinguished red light above the door.

It had not been in his plans, nor those of his guardian, to stay above a brothel. But nor could he say that he had complained too much afterwards when he found out why there was heavy traffic on those stairs, married with the heavy and mixed scents of perfume, whiskey and sweat.

The streets were still wet when he stepped out onto them, the cleaners having passed by only recently, and the sweet, tangy smell of oranges hung in the air like a played note. Welles walked towards La Maestranza, the place where the *toreros* fought bulls, went a few blocks and found a small cafe where he ordered coffee, bread and fruits.

He spread before him the *International Herald Tribune* and read while he waited. In London, Winston Churchill was warning against the threat of Germany's rearming; in Cuba, a war and a revolution were brewing; New York saw a Jewish boycott beginning of German businesses.

He ate his breakfast leisurely once it had arrived, then ordered a second one. He felt most mornings, when he awoke, inconsolably hungry, as if his insides were completely and hopelessly a chasm.

After he had finished with the paper, he took a pen from his pocket and began to write in the margins of the stories, rolling his sleeves so that he would not brush ink from the newsprint upon the cotton.

'Detective... Jim... No, Johnny...' Welles said to himself. 'That's a better name for a boy detective. Detective... No, private detective Johnny Hardy of Baltimore, who lives with his aunt Constance.'

*That will do*, thought Welles. *That's an idea. A teenaged boy detective who lives with his aunt in Baltimore. That's something I can write.*

He thought that he could write and send this one to *Adventure*. It seemed like the sort of premise it would take once he had fleshed it out into a story and given it some 'lift'. He would work out in the afternoon what was supposed to happen and to whom and when, and he would string it all along until it hung together perfectly. And in a day or so, when he was happy that it was good enough, he would send it to his man, John Clayton in Chicago, who would package it as one of his own and then forward it on for him, before sending back whatever would be his share of the fee.

He sketched out a simple, three-act structure on the back page of the newspaper, which he then removed from the rest, folded and stuck in his pocket. He left the carcass of that morning's edition on the table, then walked through the streets to the Western Union office near the city's main train station.

The inside of the office was dark and stuffy, as if someone had thrown a warm and thick woollen blanket, with slits for the odd piece of sunlight to pass through, over the building. He had come into the building off Calle Arjona, gone down a white tiled corridor with blue walls, turned, gone down some steps and entered a brown room that seemed made entirely of wood.

'*Nombre?*' The thin, punctilious clerk looked over the desk at him.

'Welles.'

'*El Americano?*' It seemed the word had spread about the young American kid who had come to Seville.

'*Si.*'

'*Un momento, por favor.*' The clerk began to look through a small stack of telegrams, clipped inside a large, leather book.

'*Primero?*'

'*Qué?*'

'*Primero.* Your first name.'

'George. George Orson Welles.'

The clerk pulled out a thin strip of paper. '*Si, si.* Passport?'

Welles handed over the document. The clerk took it, examined it and pushed over a paper for him to sign. Then he handed him a thick envelope.

'*Gracias.*'

Welles stepped back into the corridor and opened the envelope. There was a one-page note inside, nestled up against a half inch of Spanish money.

He unfolded the note: *We sold three stories. STOP. Money enclosed. STOP. Clayton. STOP.*

Welles took the money and pushed it deep into his right pocket, sticking it beneath the heavy pen. Then he folded the note, put it back into the envelope, folded that, too, and placed it in his left pocket.

He walked quickly back to his hotel, went briskly up the stairs and placed most of the money beneath the hole in the stand where the basin usually sat, carefully lifting the porcelain bowl from its usual spot. Then he sat back down on the bed, his feet stiff in the leather shoes he wore that made him sweat in the Spanish heat.

Welles shuffled the rest of the money. He pulled out a few notes

and lay them beside him on the bed. 'That's for dinner for the next two nights.' He took another two notes and put them with the pile. 'And that's in case there is someone else with me.'

What was left still felt heavy in his hand. He pinched it between his fingers and tapped it against his palm.

He stood, waiting, in Carla's bookshop an hour later, looking at shelves and shelves of brown, leather-bound books. She kept some English ones for the few tourists who came in.

There was the sound of running water and a curtain twitched at the back of the store, then moved to one side. Carla came out. Her hair was long and dark, her cheeks full. Welles blushed.

'Orson!' she called to him. 'You're back!'

Welles looked down. 'I guess I am.'

Carla nodded. 'I thought you would be gone by now, *Americano.*' She smiled. 'But you are still here.'

'I guess so.'

She beckoned him towards her with her long, angular hand, pulling him into the back of the store. 'I'm afraid I don't have any more Shakespeare for you,' she said, although there was no real note of apology in her voice. 'Why don't you try something else? A Christopher Marlowe?'

Welles breathed out. 'I want something about Spain.'

'About Spain? And you will want it in English?'

'Do you have something?'

'And you would like it written well?'

'Indeed.'

'So, you are in Seville, in my bookshop and you want something about Spain that is both well written and in English, because you do not speak Spanish? Is that true?'

25

Welles blushed again. 'Yes.'

'How about one of your modern masters? Ernest Hemingway? Have you heard of him?'

'Well, I think everyone—' He watched Carla sidle down the narrow aisle of her bookshop and disappear into the back. He waited again.

After a few moments, she came out and pressed a hardbound book into his hands.

'Here,' she said. 'He wrote this about Spain and about the... *bull-fighting.*' She said the word as if a fly had landed in her mouth.

'You don't like it?'

'I like it more than the bulls would if they knew what was happening.'

Welles looked down at the black clothbound book. The hard cover was creased in one corner and there was scuffing in places. In gold, emblazoned across the front, was Ernest Hemingway's signature. Welles held the book up in front of him and tapped the name with his finger. 'Did Hemingway write this?' he asked, his face determinedly innocent.

'You are a silly boy.'

Welles turned the book in his hands. The title *Death in the Afternoon* was written on the spine.

'I'll take it.'

Afterwards, Welles went back out into the streets of Seville where he found a cafe. He sat and read *Death in the Afternoon* for hours until the sky began to turn dark. Then, as the light began to fail, he walked back to his hotel, went up the stairs and passed the place with all the girls and lay in bed to read some more beneath a small buzzing lamp.

He went to La Maestranza the next morning and bought a ticket to the afternoon's bullfighting. It was the cheapest one he could find, and it meant he would have to sit in the *sol* section, where the sun would beat down directly into his eyes. It was a good thing, then, that he had also taken that day's *International Herald Tribune* from his neighbour, too.

He watched the men come out onto the sand in their *traje de luces*, the horns playing them into the arena. And then the bull was let out and it blinked as images of people flooded into its mind. It gasped.

Welles took a long, deep and heavy breath. He began to imagine he was reporting all this to himself, as if he was a newsman on the radio, describing something unseen to an audience.

'What am I doing here?' he intoned, remembering his time on the Dublin stage. He forced his voice lower, and he paced out the gaps between the words. 'It is, after all, a form of theatre.'

His stomach dropped at the end of the third act when the bull was killed, and it fell face first to the ground. Its blood ran thickly onto the sand. The matador, in his suit of white, silver and blue, reached over and touched the dead bull on the top of its head with the same movement and grace of an uncle petting his favourite nephew. Then he reached in and, taking a small dagger, cut through the skin of the bull's neck.

'My god,' said Welles, beneath his breath. 'Everything is here.'

He walked out afterwards onto Calle Adriano and then turned left, intending to go down by the river where the air would be at its coolest. He went and stood down there for a few moments, then turned and walked back the way he had come, and he found a small bar where he knew, from the people who had sat beside him, the matadors would come after the bullfights.

It was there, on the terrace, that he found the bullfighter he most wanted to see. It was the one who wore the white, blue and silver *traje de luces*.

Welles shuffled towards him, *Death in the Afternoon* in hands that were clasped across his stomach. 'May I sit down?'

The bullfighter looked up at him with tired eyes. He had a half-burned cigarette in one hand. 'You are *El Americano*?'

'*Si*.'

'I've heard of you.'

'It seems that everyone in Seville has.'

'What is a boy doing here by himself, so far from home?'

Welles grimaced. He deflected. 'A man's home is not where he was born but where he chooses to die.'

The bullfighter stubbed out the cigarette on a small plate. 'That's good. Who said that?'

Welles smiled. 'I did, just now.'

'You are a writer?'

'No. I'm an actor. Or I want to be.'

The bullfighter nodded. 'I am Jean-Luc.' He looked at the scepticism in Welles's face. 'My mother is French. And you are?'

'Orson Welles. George Orson Welles.'

Jean-Luc nodded. 'And you are in Seville for the bulls?'

'I am here in Europe for the culture. I am learning things.'

'And your parents are happy about this?'

Welles grimaced. He deflected. He looked at the suit that Jean-Luc still wore, and he could see that it was heavy and looked as if it would be sweltering in the heat. Jean-Luc had taken the jacket off and the shirt beneath it was drying in the sultriness of the Spanish air. There were some flecks of blood on Jean-Luc's trousers and tights.

'I would like to learn about bullfighting.'

Jean-Luc nodded. He shrugged. 'I see you have your Mr Heming-way. He's another *Americano*, no? And your Sidney Franklin?'

Welles put the book on the table. 'They are.'

Jean-Luc snorted. 'I haven't read it. I'll wait until it's in Spanish.'

'You don't seem to like it very much.'

'I don't know any *Americano* who can write well about Spain. They are not Spanish.'

'You can't learn?'

'No, you can only learn so much – 60 per cent – without get-ting onto the sand. But your Mr Hemingway has already written everything you need, no?'

'Has he?'

'I would say so. I don't know. I haven't read him.'

'You haven't?'

'No. Why would I? I live this life.'

'And if I wanted to live it?'

'Then you would have to learn it, wouldn't you?'

'How do I do that?'

'Do you have a pen?'

Welles took his pen from his pocket and handed it to Jean-Luc. The bullfighter took it in his left hand, then pulled Welles's copy of *Death in the Afternoon* to him. He opened it at the back and wrote in it for a few seconds. 'What is this?' said Welles.

'This is an address,' said Jean-Luc. 'Come here in two days at 10 a.m. And bring some money. We will teach you a thing or two about bullfighting.'

Welles went two days later, early in the morning, before the sun had reached its full height. He took a taxi to the outskirts of Seville

and then down a dusty road to a small farm. He looked through the window as the car went over a bumpy road, and he saw bulls in the fields.

A small man walked across the courtyard. He limped on both feet. He came up to Welles and stopped and stared up into the face of the tall boy.

'*El Americano?*'

'*Si.*'

'Come.' He began to lead Welles back towards the fields.

Welles cleared his throat and tugged at his clothes. 'Do I need to change?'

'*Qué?*'

'The clothes...' He fingered his shirt collar. '*Vestidos... nuevo?*'

The old man waved his hand above his head and carried on hobbling. 'No.'

They went out into a field. The grass was thin and brown, and the ground was dusty with dry soil and sand. Welles saw Jean-Luc ahead, a *muleta* over his arm.

The bullfighter walked over to him. 'I didn't think you'd come,' he said.

Welles shrugged awkwardly. 'Well, I'm here,' he replied.

'I see.'

Jean-Luc pointed to a small cart, covered in canvas with rickety wheels and horns. 'This is your bull,' he said.

Welles looked at the cart. 'Really?'

'*Si.* And this is your *muleta.*' He handed over the cloth with the stick inside. He put the stick in Welles's hand, then let the fabric drape towards the ground. 'Hold it like this.'

'OK.'

'Now, let me be the bull.' Jean-Luc walked over to the cart, took

its handles and walked fifty yards away from Welles with it. 'Are you ready?'

'Yes. I mean, *si*.'

Jean-Luc began to walk over to Welles. 'OK,' he called. 'Be ready to step to the side. And then drape the *muleta* over the head of the bull. That's me.'

'OK.'

The cart rattled as it went over a rough, dry sod in the ground. 'OK, I'm coming. I'm the bull, so I'm looking for your body. You want the bull to think the *muleta* is your body, so it's about trickery. Show them one thing and make them think that it is another. Can you do that?'

'I can.' Welles extended the *muleta* out, keeping his body to its side.

'Now, take a step back but keep the *muleta* in the same place.'

Welles shifted his feet. Jean-Luc was close now.

'It is too late for the bull to change direction at this distance. But it is also too late for you to do so, too. So, you have to stay in place.'

'I get it.'

'It is not as easy as it sounds. They are made of beef and have horns, and they are angry at you.'

'I get it.'

Jean-Luc passed Welles by and went into the *muleta*. 'Now, turn,' he said, 'and step back a few steps.'

Welles moved back. 'And now?'

'Now, I fly by you, and I will turn. And we will do this again.'

'It seems very simple.'

'It is not. There are thousands of ways to make the bull miss you. And a million ways for it to kill you.'

'I understand.'

'That you do. Now you must spend the rest of your life learning it. There is no end to that.'

It was two weeks later and Welles was being driven an hour in an old Citroën to a small town north of Seville. There were four of them crammed into the car, itself a part of the caravan that was taking Jean-Luc to his next show. It was sweaty and cramped, but there had not been enough money for the team to rent hotel rooms, so they had decided to drive there and back in the same day.

Welles felt nauseous, and he cracked open the window to smell air that was only a little sweeter or cooler than that inside the car. The *traje de luces* he wore was loose in the shoulders, built for the frame of a larger man, and he desperately wanted to drink some water. He looked at the glass bottle between his knees that he had taken from the hotel, and he put his hand on it.

'Not now,' said Jean Luc, looking over at him. 'After the event.'

'Really?'

'Really.'

'Why?'

'Just in case,' Jean-Luc replied and left it at that.

Welles had learned more of the basics behind bullfighting over two more days at the farm. And at the end of the third day, Jean-Luc had come to him and said that he could be one of the helpers at an event. Welles had enthusiastically said he would.

Jean-Luc called a week later to give him the details. He told him, 'But you will not be able to kill anything. You will just distract it with the cape. Do you understand?'

'I understand,' said Welles.

And now they were travelling together in the car.

It was a spare crowd that afternoon in the bullring. Jean-Luc led the way out onto the sand, with Welles and two other *banderilleros* following him, and he walked around the edges where that sand was packed hard and tight against the fences, and he took his *montera* off his head and held it up to the crowd.

Welles stopped as he came through the gate and looked up. There were spaces between people, gaps like broken teeth, and the chairs around the bullring went up only ten or fifteen rows, many fewer than at La Maestranza.

Jean-Luc circled back around and took hold of Welles by the elbow with a tight grip. 'Are you ready, *El Americano*?'

'*Sí.*'

The matador smiled. 'Then get ready for the bull.'

They stepped back off the sand and then a horn blew, and a bull came running out. It seemed to glower at them from where it stood, its thick body on shaking legs that seemed as thin as sticks. It rolled its head from one side to the other.

Jean-Luc and his assistants walked out onto the sand. Welles followed them.

The horn blew once more, and the startled beast ran at one of the assistants who, as quickly as he could, sprinted thirty or so feet to the safety of the fences. The bull ran into that fence and there was a dull but violent thud, before it ran off in a different direction.

Now, it went for a second assistant, who flurried a *capote* around him, then also ran for the safety of the *barrera*.

Welles looked over at the first assistant, who was now coming back from behind the fence and gesticulating in his direction.

'*Vamos, vamos!*'

The other assistants began to yell. Welles looked around and

realised too late that the bull was only fifteen feet or so from him. He turned and ran, dropping his *muleta* to the floor.

His feet slipped a little in the slippers, and he lost one of them as he covered the twenty or so yards to the fence. The thudding of the bull's hooves against the dense sand grew deeper and louder.

Welles reached the fence and put one hand on it and swung himself around, smashing his back against the fence on the adjoining side.

A sharp pain sliced across the back of his calf and he instinctively pulled his leg up, rolling into a ball then flopping into the safety of the *callejón*.

Welles was taken to the infirmary afterwards, where the doctor, between sucking on a dirty cigarette, put two or three stitches into his flesh. Welles sweated in pain and drank liberally from a bottle of wine that someone had brought in for him.

Jean-Luc entered. '*Está bien?*'

The doctor dropped the cigarette on the floor and crushed it beneath his shoe. '*Sí.*' He looked from Jean-Luc to Welles. '*El Americano?*'

Jean-Luc nodded. '*El Americano.*'

The doctor laughed, then slapped Welles on the leg. '*Se recuperará.*'

Jean-Luc laughed.

Jean-Luc sat down on the wooden table Welles was on after the doctor had left. 'You were lucky, my friend,' he said.

'Lucky?'

'Of course.'

'Well, I guess the wound could have been worse.'

Jean-Luc scoffed. 'No, most *torero* wait their entire career for

an injury. Now that you have one, your career must have started. Maybe you will be an immortal like your Sidney Franklin or your Ernest Hemingway.'

'I doubt it. I must be the worst bullfighter in history.'

'In that case, that is how they will remember you. As the worst bullfighter in history. Congratulations, *El Americano* – you are now immortal!'

Welles put his head back and roared with laughter. Some blood from his leg dripped onto the floor.

# 3

# MURMURINGS OF WAR
# (1936 TO 1937)

The long black truck threaded its way through Madrid, its wheels rumbling over the cobbled, dry streets. The men inside had kept the windows up so no one could look in and see who they were, and the temperature had risen.

Fernando Condés, in the front passenger seat, swallowed. His throat was dry. He tapped his hands on his leg, and he looked at the darkness outside, the city lit by lamps here and there. Then he turned and looked to the men beside him.

Gradually, the truck went tightly through the centre of the city and headed towards its northern parts. The group had struck out on its first two targets – neither was at home – so it was headed now to the third.

It was a few hours past midnight when they pulled up outside the apartment building at Calle de Velázquez 89. The dark-suited men got out and stood in a huddle.

'Is this it?' asked one.

'Yes.'

'Are you sure?'

'Yes.'

'Are you *sure*?'

'Yes.'

There were two policemen in the doorway. One of them reached down and put his hand on his gun, quietly undoing the clasp.

'Relax, friend,' Condés said, walking up to him, showing his papers. 'I'm with the Civil Guard.'

The policeman looked at the papers, then at the group. He read the situation. 'Who are they?'

'They are with me.'

'They are?'

'Yes.' Condés looked at him and his colleague. 'Tell me, do you love Spain? Are you a good Spaniard?'

The policemen looked at each other. They looked at the fourteen men in front of them. They read the situation. 'Yes.'

'Good.' Condés turned and nodded his head to the group. He turned back to the policemen. 'We're going up,' he said. 'Is *he* in?'

'Yes.'

'Thank you.'

The group went upstairs. Condés knocked on the door. He waited a few seconds, then knocked again. He was about to rap his hand against the wood for a third time when a small, thin voice spoke to him from the other side. It belonged to an elderly woman.

'Who is it?'

'Police. We're here to do a search.'

'At this time?'

'We work all the time.'

'Can you come back?'

'If you don't open up, we will have to break in.'

'Please wait.'

'Not for long.'

There were many people inside the apartment, but the one they were looking for was the politician José Calvo Sotelo. The people behind the door – his maid and his cook – woke him, and he went and looked over the balcony to the van below.

Calvo Sotelo went to the door. He motioned for his cook and his maid to move away. 'It *is* the police,' he reassured them. Dread began to settle in his stomach like sediment.

He opened the door. The group went inside. Most of them pushed past him and went to search the apartment. Someone disconnected the telephone cord from the wall and pulled a monarchist flag from the table and threw it to the floor. Calvo Sotelo swallowed, looked at it.

'Stay here,' Condés said.

'What is this?'

'Stay here.'

'You need to tell me what is going on.'

'We have orders for your arrest. The General Director for Security wants you.'

'Why?'

'He wants to talk to you.'

'I am a parliamentarian, and I am immune. And you come to my house?' Calvo Sotelo gestured around him. 'I think I need to speak to the General Director for Security right now on the phone.'

Condés looked at him. 'No.'

'Who are you?'

'I'm with the Civil Guard.'

'Papers.'

Condés handed over the papers. Calvo Sotelo looked at them.

He looked up, and he saw his wife and daughter, shaking, standing next to one of the men. 'Don't worry,' he said. 'If they're telling the truth, I will be back in an hour. The government will do nothing against me.'

His wife stepped forwards. 'Don't go with them.'

Calvo Sotelo looked at Condés. 'I have to.'

Condés spoke to her. 'He has to.'

The group began to come back into the room. Calvo Sotelo looked at his wife. 'Pack me a briefcase,' he said.

'Don't go.'

'I have to.' He looked at Condés. 'I need to get dressed.'

'One of my men will go with you.'

'Really?'

Condés said nothing. One of the group went with Calvo Sotelo to his bedroom where he got dressed. He went to the bedrooms of his other three children, still asleep, and kissed them. He kissed his wife. He took the briefcase she had prepared for him. He kissed his daughter.

'Now?' he asked Condés.

'Now.'

Four or five of the group went ahead, with Calvo Sotelo in the middle, a hand firmly on his elbow. The rest of the group went down the stairs behind them.

Calvo Sotelo stopped at the doorway. He looked at the van. He breathed in the warm air of the night, and he looked over and saw the policemen.

'They are taking me under arrest,' he said. 'I have not been able to talk on the phone.'

The hand was back on his elbow, and Calvo Sotelo was led to the van. 'In here,' a voice said. 'The middle bench.'

Calvo Sotelo sat on the bench. Men in uniform sat on either side of him. Some more sat behind. Condés sat in the front. They said nothing, and the van drove off.

It had taken less than fifteen minutes for the group to enter the apartment building, pick up Calvo Sotelo and get him into the van. Now, they were driving once more through the warm city night.

They drove for a few minutes down Calle de Velázquez. As they came to Calle de Ayala, one of the men sitting behind Calvo Sotelo reached down, took out his gun and shot the politician twice in the head.

The assassination of José Calvo Sotelo by leftists was the biggest spark of many to light the Spanish Civil War. Calvo Sotelo had been a monarchist, the leader of the political opposition and a member of the forces seeking to undermine and ultimately do away with Spain's new democratic government. He had also been a fascist. After being part of the nation's previous dictatorship and a leading figure in its administration, he had gone into exile in Portugal and France before returning under amnesty in 1934, becoming a leading light in the 'National Block', a project that sought to unite the right-leaning elements of Spanish society. Seemingly aware that a rebellion was fomenting, Calvo Sotelo was poised to become a leading figure in whatever new dictatorship would rise in Spain.

His assassination, on the night of 13 July 1936 in Madrid, was seen widely as retaliation for that of police officer José Castillo by fascists hours earlier. Castillo had been assassinated in the early evening as he left his home in Madrid to walk to work.

These events followed weeks and months of tensions throughout Spain between its widely reviled leftist government and the opposing forces of the monarchists, military, landowners and Catholic Church.

A coup had been forming for months, but the killings of Calvo Sotelo and Castillo fired the starting pistol. In Morocco, General Franco joined the revolt, with his regiment seizing control before heading to mainland Spain. The Republican government managed to hold back the initial coup, and a stalemate formed between the two broad sides.

It was the beginning of the Spanish Civil War.

But in Florida, there were other ghosts in the mind of Hemingway.

Less than a year before, a hurricane had ripped through the state, killing hundreds whose bodies lay bloating for days and weeks in the hot sun. Many of the families had been living in huts, living hand to mouth, as the fathers and husbands went to build a bridge and a highway. They had been jobless, and the government had sent them south to work. The hurricane passed through them.

Hemingway was there, reporting and helping to recover the corpses. He had known many of the dead.

He had always remained apolitical, writing for neither one side nor the other. But what he saw in the temperature and the heat shunted something within him.

The dead had been there in the mangroves, their bodies now too big to fill the clothes that they had worn before like sheets. Hemingway went with others, and they wore gas masks to stem the rotting-flesh smell, and they would lash four or five of the bodies together with strong ropes, the fibres burning and rubbing the skin from their hands, so that those bodies would not be washed out to sea. Hemingway blinked in the heat and the sun, and he swallowed and drank even more than he normally did, and he pushed his thoughts down deep inside him, so they were buried enough.

He had known them at Josie Grunt's and at Sloppy Joe's in Key

West. He knew them when they had been drunk, and when they had been sober, and when those who had been fighters had fought amongst themselves. He had known the good ones and the bad ones. He had not known them all, but he saw enough that he felt he had.

'Where are the buzzards?' a person beside him asked, crying. 'Where are the buzzards!?'

He wanted to say something wise. He wanted to say, *There is too much death for even the buzzards.*

He looked at the person beside him and he raised the gas mask from his face, the rubber squeaking against his wet skin and pulling at his rough beard. 'The wind scared them,' he said.

He saw a woman. He saw what had been a woman. It was now just a body. He saw another one. He turned them over in the sun. He had known both of them. They had been sisters. They had run a sandwich place and a filling station that he went – *had gone* – to.

Someone asked him afterwards how they were. He seemed to not understand the question. But he understood his answer. The thought pulled itself through his mind like the extrication of a thorn. *What good were they?* he thought. *They were well fed, well housed, well treated. I suppose now that they are well dead.*

He drank more. He wrote.

He wrote for *New Masses*:

During the war, troops and sometimes individual soldiers who incurred the displeasure of their superior officers, were some-times sent into positions of extreme danger and kept there repeat-edly until they were no longer problems. I do not believe anyone, knowingly, would send US war veterans into any such positions in time of peace.

The Florida winds blew through his house. Tears fell onto the paper. He shook them off, carried on writing.

'But the Florida Keys,' he wrote,

in hurricane months, in the matter of casualties recorded during the building of the Florida East Coast Railway to Key West, when nearly a thousand men were killed by hurricanes, can be classed as such a position. And ignorance has never been accepted as an excuse for murder or for manslaughter.

His mind was still shaken when the Spanish started fighting. He slipped in and out of dark moods, and he talked of suicide. The Spanish Civil War became a larger and larger story in newsprint. He worried about his weight, starting training as a boxer again. He lost ten pounds.

He wrote *Green Hills of Africa*. He began to get lost in his own myth. He struggled to reconcile who he was with who the world wanted to see. He struggled to be who *he* wanted it to see.

He began to resent Pauline. He began to resent age. He had already begun to resent Gus and the money.

The war was there. He thought again about the war. He wanted to go.

The public turned on him. They turned on his books. He was the most prominent writer in America. They wanted him to stand for something. He stood for nothing. He began writing a crime thriller, cobbled together from old pieces, called *To Have and Have Not*.

He wrote to Maxwell Perkins, his publisher, in September. He thought the war would not last long. He needed to finish the book first. He told him he would leave the manuscript in a vault so it could be published if he died. He said there were fiction stories, too.

Perkins could publish them if he needed to make money if Hemingway died.

He wrote to Perkins again a month later. He said he had to go to Spain. He said there was no big hurry, that the war would continue for a long time and, besides, Madrid was cold in December. He spoke of the money he had sent over there. He said they would have made him a corporal in their army if he had sent more. He criticised Franco's strategies, his manoeuvres.

He thought of home. He thought of what America was doing. He wanted his country to stay out of another European war. He wrote for *Esquire* and called it a 'hell broth'. The US had no need of it, he said. But he saw what was happening in Spain. His mind started to shift.

He drank more and his eyesight was bad. He told people he could no longer go into the boxing ring but could still fight in the street. He drank too much. Even Pauline told him that.

The war loomed closer. He thought more about it. He wanted to go.

The North American Newspaper Alliance reached out. It offered him $1,000 for just over a thousand words. It offered him $500 per cable from the war. It was the most any reporter or writer was being offered.

He finished *To Have and Have Not*.

He decided he could have the war.

He knew it was a bad war in which no one was right. He cared about people, and he wanted to see no one suffer, even if suffering was noble.

He knew a writer called Harry Sylvester. He told him that it was a bad war. He questioned the right wing. He questioned the left wing. He told Sylvester that it was not his business, but he would make it so.

He wrote to Sidney Franklin and persuaded him to go and be his driver.

He went to Sloppy Joe's one night where he met Wife #3 – Martha. She stood at the bar in a black dress. There were beads of sweat in her hair.

'You're Hemingway,' she said. It was not a question.

Hemingway nodded. 'And you?'

'Gellhorn. Martha Gellhorn.' She dragged on her cigarette. She had wanted to meet him. She wanted him to think that she did *not* want to meet him.

Hemingway scoped her out. 'I've heard of you.'

'Some people have.'

Hemingway wiped at his stubble. He looked over to two people, a young man and an older woman, staring at him and Gellhorn. 'You have fans?'

'Not like you.'

'Who are they?'

'That's my brother and my mother.'

'A family affair?'

'We're on vacation.'

'The trouble you've seen, eh?'

'Very funny. So you *have* read my book.' Again, it was not a question.

'Oh, I've read more than one of them.'

She stubbed out the cigarette. 'You haven't asked if I've read any of yours.'

'Everyone has read Hemingway.'

'Everyone?'

'They either have, say they have or deny they have.'

'Funny.'

He looked over her, standing at the bar. He felt that she did not

belong there but also that it would have been incomplete without her. 'Are you going anywhere?' he asked.

'Tonight?'

'You know what I mean.'

She lit another cigarette, and she nodded at him. 'Spain. I figure I'd better get there before the war dies out or it kills everyone. You?'

'Same.'

'Then why aren't you there now?'

'I've a book to finish, then I'll go.'

'Maybe I'll see you there, Mr Hemingway.'

He knocked back a shot. 'Good try, Miss...'

'Gellhorn.'

'... Miss Gellhorn, but I'm married.'

She shrugged. 'That's nice. I might try that myself one day.'

Hemingway turned back to the bar. He signalled for another drink. He wiped at his mouth again, then rubbed his hand down his dirty shirt and onto his soiled white shorts. He looked back once more at Gellhorn. 'I've heard other things about you,' he said.

'Like what?'

'That you had an affair with H. G. Wells. That you lived in Paris, but no one knew you, and you knew no one. That you have the patronage of Eleanor Roosevelt. Does any of that jibe?'

'It jibes. Parts of it.'

'Which parts?'

'No, I didn't have an affair with H. G. Wells, although I think he would've appreciated it if I did. Yes, I lived in Paris, but everyone was posing as the next Hemingway or Fitzgerald, and the people I knew there were those I wanted to know – the best people. And, yes, Eleanor is a dear friend.'

'I also hear that you can't find a magazine to help you get to Spain.'

'Don't believe everything you hear, Mr Hemingway.'

'I didn't say I believed it. I just said I heard it.'

'Is there anything else you've heard about me?'

'Those things? I'll tell you about them in Spain.'

'Well, then, I'll meet you in Madrid when you get off the train, Mr Hemingway.'

Gellhorn stayed in Florida for a fortnight longer than her brother and her mother so that she could tighten her bond with Hemingway. She stayed in the same rooms, and she said that she was working on a novel. She spent time with Hemingway and his wife. She spoke about stories with him, men with her. She waited while Ernest and Pauline went to Miami for a few days, then followed them.

Pauline could see the rhyme of history. She had taken Ernest from Hadley, now Martha was taking him from her.

Gellhorn saw Hemingway in Miami. She ate dinner with him, then they took a train north. They split off from each other in Jacksonville eight hours later, and she headed away from him to St Louis.

Hemingway walked her to her train. He reached over and held her hand. It was taut and rough, her skin bristling against his own. He gripped her small, tight fingers with his own large ones, and he rubbed his thumb against the back of her knuckles. Gellhorn looked down at the hand, then at him.

She opened the carriage door and stepped up. She leaned down. Hemingway put his hands on either side of her face and leaned in, then kissed her on the forehead. 'Goodbye, daughter,' he told her.

'Shall I see you in Spain?' she asked.

Hemingway nodded. 'Spain,' he said, simply.

The war did little to come to Orson Welles in New York. He was twenty-one years old and working the stages and radio booths across the city, his wife Virginia at home. He left early in the morning from their apartment on West 14th Street and he ran from one end of Manhattan to the other, auditioning here, acting there and then he would go each night to Harlem with John Houseman, coming home only to barely sleep, then head out again.

The pair of them were working for the Federal Theatre Project, part of the New Deal to reinvigorate the economy. After an all-black, voodoo version of *MacBeth* with the Negro Theatre Unit, Welles and Houseman had turned their attention to an Americanised version of the French farce *Un chapeau de paille d'Italie*.

Welles needed music, and he asked the composer Marc Blitzstein to write every piece.

Blitzstein went to see Welles at Maxine Elliott's Theatre. He came in at the end of a rehearsal and he saw Welles sitting in the third row, a bowl of vanilla ice cream in one hand, watching the players on stage.

The lights went on, the stage emptied and Blitzstein went down to the front and slipped behind Welles. He could see the amphetamine twitching of Welles's neck.

Welles waved at actor Joseph Cotten as he left the stage. 'Good work, Joe!' he called out. Cotten waved back, then slipped into the darkness.

Blitzstein put a hand on the twitching shoulder in front of him. 'Orson?'

Welles turned, raising an eyebrow. He looked up and down at his visitor. 'Marc!' he said, getting to his feet. 'You're here!'

'I am.'

'They let you in?' Welles laughed. 'Come sit with me.'

Blitzstein went back into the aisle, came down a row and moved over to where Welles was sitting. The theatre was, apart from some grips moving around, completely empty.

Welles sat down again and stretched out. The skin around his eyes was taut. He yawned, and then he put the cold bowl of ice cream to his forehead. 'Thank you for coming,' he said. Blitzstein saw that Welles's suit looked rumpled, as if it had been travelled in for more miles than it was meant to. The white collar was stained and grimy, and the green paisley tie was askew. His black hair was long and unkempt, brushing the collar of the shirt, and his fingers were stained brown from what Blitzstein assumed were the cigars.

'You wanted me?'

'That's true.' Although Welles was young, Blitzstein thought it was the most unique voice, like a rope being wound tightly around a stone column. Welles coughed. 'We need music for the production.'

'That was my understanding.'

'You've read the book?'

'The latest version. And you're now calling it *Horse Eats Hat*? Is that right?'

'That's good enough. We haven't changed much since then, I think.' Welles took a spoonful of the ice cream and put it, dripping, into his mouth. Some of it dropped on his tie, and he brushed at it with a thumb that he then put in his mouth. 'So you know what I need?'

'I think so.'

'And what would that be?' Welles stopped, the spoon hanging in his mouth.

'Two long pieces of continuity, three overtures, the horse ballet and several songs.'

Welles looked ahead. He began nodding in a regulated tempo.

'Yes, that sounds about right.' A second or two went by. 'Yes, that's correct. Can you do it?'

'I can.'

'Good.' Welles carried on nodding.

Blitzstein sat back in his seat. 'You have a lot on.'

Welles sat back beside Blitzstein. He closed his eyes again and pinched his nose. His voice went down an octave as if preparing for a performance. 'Of course,' he said, as if that was all the explanation he needed to give.

Blitzstein waited. He knew that you had to wait and let an actor fill the silence in worry.

Welles clinked the spoon against the bowl. 'I will be on stage, in a drama this time, in October. It's called *Ten Million Ghosts*. I'm also directing that with Houseman as well as directing this. I also have to do two to three radio shows a day to keep this whole thing on the road. And the guys at CBS want me to play *The Shadow* next.' He laughed and rubbed at his eyebrow with the same thumb he had just put in his mouth, then ruffled his hair.

'That's a lot.'

'There's a lot going on everywhere.'

Welles put his hand on Blitzstein's arm and leaned over, so their faces were almost touching. 'Tell me something,' he said. 'You've been to Spain, Marc?'

'No, but I've been in Berlin. I've seen what's going on there, though. I only know a little about Spain.'

'But what do you think is happening if you had to say anything about it?'

'There's a war going on between one side and another. And one side will devolve eventually into a bunch of other sides, and they'll all fight amongst and against each other.'

Welles's face turned grave. 'Yes. And do you know what happens at the end?'

'No.'

'Fascism.' He looked sad. 'Of everything I've seen in the world, the one thing I'm certain of in Spain is that there is no hope of anything but fascism.'

# 4

# CONTEMPORARY HISTORIANS
# (1937)

The tall blonde woman with the long legs stepped up to the border between France and Spain and, without hesitation, crossed out of one country and into another.

It had taken Martha Gellhorn a great deal of time and effort to get to that point, just south of Andorra, and she knew that none of that time and effort had been expended on her behalf by the man who insisted on being addressed as 'Papa'. She had been given a letter from *Collier's* that said she was their correspondent and then she had waited for weeks in Paris for a visa. Eventually, she had gone to Toulouse, consulted an old map and then walked to the border after it became clear that that visa would not arrive.

She had walked for hours, and her feet were sore in her boots, and she had been hot for all of the afternoon before the day had begun its cooling slide into dusk, a time that she thought best to cross the border. On Spanish soil, she looked behind her, to the ten yards into France, and thought that not much felt different in the handful of steps that had taken her from that place and into this new one.

The night air was cool, and she breathed in her first breath of

Spain, then let it out, watched the faint tendrils of steam from her mouth dissipate into nothing and suddenly felt tired. All that was left was to somehow get to Valencia, then Madrid, find Hemingway and report on a war.

There was a farmer a few miles into Spain who drove her from the foot of the Pyrenees to Girona. From there, she took an unheated train filled with recruits into Barcelona as snow fell outside in blossoms of pink and white.

*By eight*, she later wrote, *the trees were of glass and the fields were white and the snow blew flat over the land.*

The city was full of young men with hope on their faces for a good war to fight and die for. She hated all of it. She loved all of them.

She stayed there a few nights, saw a factory, missed out on a bombardment while sleeping. She fell in platonic love with all of those boys. She wanted them to win. She knew that they would win. And then she caught herself in her thinking and knew that she somehow needed to go to Valencia.

She found a truck taking munitions there and hitched a lift, and that was how she found herself four hours later about to share a car to Madrid with Sidney Franklin.

Franklin was still in pain from the wound. It had come a month before, from a horn near Mexico City, and was refusing to heal. So he had used that extra time in Paris to rest while waiting for his visa. He and Papa had come from New York on the same boat, and Papa managed right away to get his papers for Spain, but the authorities in France had viewed Franklin with some suspicion, so they had made him wait over a week before they eventually waved him through.

He also had with him all the supplies that Papa had wanted: six Spanish hams, ten kilograms of coffee, four kilograms of butter, 100 kilograms of tinned marmalade and another 100 kilograms of assorted fruits. And, somehow, he had managed to bring it all with him across the border and down into Valencia where he was waiting for the Republicans to give him another car so he could finish transporting it all down to Madrid, where he knew that Papa was staying at the Hotel Florida.

He dozed, waiting, in a small office. Someone had been by a few hours before and told him that they would send him when they had one other person to sit in the truck with him. And so, Franklin, his bushy red hair pushed under a beret, wrapped an overcoat around himself and tried to sleep on one of the wooden benches.

He was dreaming, thinking about sand and boys and Spain and Brooklyn when a rough hand shook his shoulder. He startled and his neck twinged, and he felt the stitches around his wound pull and stretch as he jolted. The hand shook his shoulder once more, pulling him completely out of sleep. Franklin sat up, tenderly, leaning more on one side than the other, and rubbed his eyes.

'She will go with you,' the voice said again in Spanish.

'Who?'

'The woman.'

Franklin looked across the office and saw Gellhorn. She had pulled her hair back into a ponytail and her face was dirty, and he could not help but be repulsed by the scuffed-up boots, grey flannel trousers and windcheater she wore. He was surprised, but not pleased, to see her.

'Hi, Sidney,' she said.

'Hi, Martha.'

'Looks like we're riding together.'

Twenty minutes later, Gellhorn and Franklin were riding to Madrid, the two of them heading through the rough streets of Valencia, the truck's wheels jolting over cobbles, in the cool night air.

Neither was given to talking. They had known each other briefly, only through Hemingway, in Florida and New York. Franklin loved Pauline. He saw Gellhorn for what she meant, and Gellhorn repelled him. To Gellhorn, Franklin was small and insignificant and an annoyance.

It was about an hour into the ride before Franklin said anything of substance. The road dipped a little and he sped up on the smooth tarmac, and they flew past a sign for a town named 'BECHDEL'.

'Are you going to see *him*?' asked Franklin.

'Who's *him*?' replied Gellhorn.

'Papa.'

'I'm here to report on a war.'

'But you're going to see *him*?'

'Aren't we all going to see *him* at some point?'

Franklin took his eyes off the road. He looked over at Gellhorn. 'You know, I am very good friends with Pauline. I like her very much.'

'That's nice. She needs some good girlfriends.'

Franklin turned his eyes back to the road. 'I like her.'

'I'm sure you do. So do I. She's nice.'

'She let you be a guest in her house.'

Gellhorn looked out of the window. 'Can I take an orange?'

'No.' Franklin went quiet as he thought a little. He changed his mind. 'OK, you can take one.'

Gellhorn put one foot on the seat and pushed herself up and leaned over into the back where she reached into one of the crates and took out an orange. She sat back and began to peel it, leaving

the rind on the dashboard of the car. Once she had peeled the whole thing, she opened the window, took the rind and threw it out into the night.

She sniffed the air. 'It's the queerest thing,' she said, looking at Franklin.

He looked back. 'What is?'

She took a segment of orange and put it into her mouth. 'That these Spanish oranges have such a rich perfume that the air just fills with it.'

He tapped the window. 'This, here, is where they grow them. That's what you can smell.'

Gellhorn nodded. 'I know. It smells like a wedding.'

'Why are you here, Martha?'

'I told you, Sidney. I'm here to report on a war.'

'Are you here to take a husband?'

'Absolutely not.' She pulled another segment from the orange and ate it. 'Do you want some?'

'No, thank you.'

'Because he's already married.'

'That observation has not escaped me.'

'But you're still here.'

'I have a job to do. Listen, the western democracies have two commanding obligations, as far as I see it: they must save their honour by assisting a young, attacked fellow democracy.'

'And the other?'

'They have to save their own skins, by fighting Hitler and Mussolini, at once, in Spain. If they wait, the cost in human suffering will be unimaginably greater.'

Franklin looked ahead, nodded. 'Do you have family, Martha?'

'My brother and my mother.'

'Your father?'

'He died last year.'

Franklin looked at her. There was a gleam at the bottom of her eyes. She turned her head and wiped at her tears. 'I'm sorry,' Franklin said.

Gellhorn was quiet for a time. Eventually, she murmured something.

'I'm sorry,' Franklin said, again.

Gellhorn cleared her throat. She coughed and swallowed her spit. 'You? Do you have family?'

'Back in Brooklyn, sure.'

'And you are not with them?'

'No.'

'Why is that?'

Franklin looked out through the windscreen and at the full lights of the car that lit up the road ahead of them. He saw the pure light shift into more granular patterns, and he heard the rasp and grind of the thin tyres on the gravel in front of them. 'I live here in Spain, mostly,' he said.

'I guess they don't understand you.'

'They understand me pretty well. That's why I'm here,' he said. He shifted in his seat. 'Since we're sharing, my old man was a cop, and his friends caught me with someone a long time ago, in a place where people like me go to meet other people like us. And he found out and he hit me so hard that I was unconscious for two days. And so my mother gave me some money, enough for a ticket. I went to Mexico, then here.'

'It seems like we have much in common,' Gellhorn said. She reached over and tapped her long dirty fingers on the back of Franklin's hand.

'That is a thought that I have not had,' said Franklin.

At the same time in Madrid, America's second most celebrated author was looking for his friend.

John Dos Passos had trailed Hemingway into Spain. He knew the country well, and he had lived there, and he supported *la causa*. But he was deeply troubled by the fractures running through it.

But mostly he was troubled by José Robles, his translator, whose letters had dried up like a puddle in the summer heat. The last one had arrived weeks before. Then nothing.

Now, he walked through the doors of the Hotel Florida where the first thing he saw was Hemingway, there with the documentary filmmaker Joris Ivens and the poet Archie MacLeish. The three sat behind a low table, Hemingway in the middle. They were laughing and smiling. Dos Passos knew them. They were all friends. In New York, they had decided amongst themselves to form a company called Contemporary Historians to make a film, *The Spanish Earth*, about *la causa*.

But now Dos Passos was late to the party.

It was Hemingway who saw him first, but Papa had not reacted and instead had let Dos Passos come to him. As Dos Passos crossed the floor of the lobby, Hemingway turned more in his direction, stood, lumbered over and then grabbed his hand firmly and pulled it towards him.

'Dos, you're here!' Hemingway exclaimed, then turned to the rest of the lobby. 'He made it, at last!' he called to them.

'I'm here, Hem.'

'You are! Do you want a drink? We have some brandy.'

'Brandy will be fine.'

'Come, Dos.' Hemingway began to shepherd him towards his

crowd. 'Come on, come with me. I need a good friend here with me in Spain.'

Dos Passos looked at the crowd, all of them eager to please Hemingway. 'I'm sure you do, Hem.' He looked closely at his friend in profile and saw the jaw that was beginning to sag and the skin that was beginning to turn pallid. He thought he could see some yellow in the whites of Hemingway's eyes. 'Are you well, Hem?' he asked him as they walked.

'Never better, Dos. I'm in love and in a war.'

'You're in love?'

'Of course, Dos. Of course.'

'Where's Pauline?'

Hemingway bristled and fell out of step for a second. 'Not here, Dos. Not here. I left her in Paris. This war here in Spain is too dangerous for her, and you know that she has our boys.'

Dos Passos nodded. 'Of course, Hem.'

Hemingway stopped at the sofa where he saw Ivens. 'Joris, Dos is here.'

'I can see,' Ivens said in his thick Dutch accent.

Hemingway turned back to Dos Passos. 'What did you bring with you, Dos?'

'I'm looking for José. Have you seen him?'

Hemingway looked around. 'The translator? No.'

'*My* translator. No one's seen him for weeks.'

Hemingway shrugged. 'I don't know, Dos,' he said. He looked at Ivens, then back to Dos Passos. 'Joris says we need to talk about the film.'

'I need to find José first.'

'The film first, Dos. We need to talk about the film.'

Dos Passos looked around the lobby. 'I need to get checked in,' he said.

Hemingway looked at the small bag carried by Dos Passos. 'Did you bring much with you?'

'Some chocolate. Some oranges we bought on the way down.'

Hemingway laughed. 'You're no good for this, Dos,' he said, with a guffaw. 'This is a war, and you seem to be a terrible hunter. You're going to die here if you don't stand next to me.'

'We'll see, Hem. Now, who can I speak to about José?'

'I've no idea, Dos. No idea.'

'See you later, Hem.'

Dos Passos turned and, like a man striding through his garden to look for a specific flower, he picked his way across the lobby to the reception desk.

It was dusk when Gellhorn and Franklin arrived in Madrid, and the pair went straight to Gran Via, where they knew Hemingway would be waiting at Chicote's.

Gellhorn had heard about it before the war. It was the type of place that Franklin might have known intimately. It had been, before the whole mess, a bar where the elegant young men of the city would come to drink cocktails. But times had changed, and it had since been requisitioned by the government as a haunt for journalists.

There was a guard on the door who refused to let them in until Franklin said the word 'Hemingway', and then the door was opened and they were guided down the few steps from the street to the hard cement floor that had once been filled with wooden tables and chairs since pushed to one side. It prompted immediately in Gellhorn the feeling of being on the New York subway at 5 p.m. or in the middle of Times Square or struggling to find one's platform during the busiest times at Grand Central Station.

Chicote's was a single room with a bar at one end. The place

was heated with the temperature of bodies pushed up close to one another, and the air was adulterated with the pungency of people's breath and the smell of overheated skin. The lighting was that of many dim lightbulbs, yellowish in hue, that were still not enough to illuminate the room. She felt that it must have been like falling asleep while fully awake.

She heard the voice first, and it was louder and higher than what might have been expected, and it paused only here and there for the laughter of others to break in, and she knew then that it was *him*.

Gellhorn left Franklin behind – she was happy for that – and she moved her way through the crowd, stepping between others. She felt a hand take hold of her backside, and she reached down and got one of its fingers between her thumb and forefinger and pressed down hard on the nail. There was a yelp, and the hand snapped back.

She saw his face then, and she remembered it from New York, and she saw the self-satisfaction in it that had so drawn her to him in Florida, and she saw that that same quality had risen to its surface so that it had become all of him.

'Hemingway,' she said, her voice firm.

He saw her at that moment and he slid out of the booth he was in and rose to his feet. His shirt collar was undone and the khaki trousers he wore were unpressed, and his shoes were shoes for the street and not for a war. But she allowed herself to feel happy to see him.

He came to her with his arms out. 'I see you,' he said. 'I see you, daughter!'

She looked into his face as he put his big hands on her shoulders, and then he leaned over and kissed her on the forehead. 'I knew you would get here,' he said, and then he turned to the crowd and he roared, 'I fixed it so that she could get here!'

She handed him her knapsack. 'Take this,' she said, 'and get me a drink. Then you can say that you did something for me!'

Weeks ticked by, and John Dos Passos was still looking for José Robles. No one knew where he was. They could tell you where he had been, and what he had been doing, but there was no sign of his location.

He went to the university in Valencia where Robles had taught but found only silence. It was the same with their mutual friends, the city's newspapers, the War Ministry Robles had worked for. Dos Passos asked in all the bars and he asked the soldiers but found only whispers of rumours.

He found that Robles had been translating for the Russians in Madrid, working with a general called Gorev. That general was now somewhere in the north, on the front lines against Franco. Still, no one knew where Robles was.

He took more time. He ignored *The Spanish Earth*. He and Hemingway bristled at each other.

He went to see Robles's wife. She let him into the house. She looked around the streets. She sat him down at the table. She gave him a glass of wine. She looked much older, but her eyes still held the flash of black he remembered.

'Where is José?' Dos Passos asked.

'I don't know.'

'I know. No one knows.'

'He's gone.'

Dos Passos nodded. 'He was working for the War Ministry, as a translator? That's what I understand. He was working for them, and they sent him to the Russians. Some general?'

'He never said much. He didn't want to.'

'Why?'

'He wanted to keep us safe. He never really trusted Russia.'

'He didn't trust the Russians? Why?'

'No, not the Russians. He didn't trust *Russia*. The state. He said once they were murderers in different clothes. But he loved Gorev.'

'Gorev is gone now, though. He's on the front somewhere. Up in the Basque country.'

She nodded. She went to pour more wine for Dos Passos. His glass was still full. 'You need to go from here, John,' she said, quietly.

'What happened?'

'They came here one night, and they took him.'

'Who did?'

She shrugged. 'Who knows? Our side, their side. You can't be sure sometimes.'

'What did they look like?'

'That's a dangerous question now.'

Dos Passos stopped, thought. 'When was this?'

'A few weeks ago.'

'And they never brought him back?'

'No, he never came back.'

Dos Passos took a car and drove out to meet Hemingway. He and Ivens were following the farmers. He watched from the car as Hemingway pointed to the landscape with equipment in his arms that he placed on the floor before turning back. Then Hemingway stopped, cocked his head and stared long and hard at Dos Passos. He raised his hand.

Dos Passos climbed out of the car. 'You joining us?' asked Hemingway. The air was cold. 'We could use a good man like yourself.'

'Hem, I need something from you. We need to talk.'

'What do you need, Dos?'

Dos Passos motioned for Hemingway to come with him. They moved from the cameras and from Ivens, and they turned their backs to everyone and stepped around to the other side of the car. Dos Passos put his hand on Hemingway's arm, and he whispered because of the still wind. They walked a bit further until they were out of earshot.

Hemingway looked back at the others, then he looked to Dos Passos. 'That's a hell of a distance,' he said. 'Something must really be troubling you.'

'Something is.'

'What is it?'

'I'm not sure who to trust around here.'

'You can trust Joris.'

'I know. But there's a lot of games being played here. Too many open ears. People are afraid.'

'I'm not.'

'You should be.'

Hemingway stopped and put his hands on his belt. He looked at Dos Passos with clear eyes. 'This is a new, strange kind of war,' he said, with a firm voice. 'I believe so much, almost as much as I can learn.'

'What do you believe?'

'It is as simple as light against dark. There are no more than two sides – the monarchists and the Republicans, which we call *la causa*.'

'And what do you want to happen?'

'I want our country and the English to ignore this non-intervention treaty, much like Italy and Germany are. I want them to support *la causa*.'

Dos Passos looked at his friend, and he knew then that Hemingway

was a puffed-up fool when it came to Spain. He snorted. 'They will pull this country apart,' Dos Passos said, 'and the monarchists will crush the Republicans if they can and make them suffer for years if they can't. And if the Republicans win, they will turn on each other eventually like dogs in a pit.'

'You're a cynic, Dos. What is it that you've come to ask me?'

'I still can't find José Robles. You were a reporter. You speak some version of Spanish. Help me find him.'

Hemingway shook his head. 'We have a film to make here,' he said. 'Go back to Madrid, Dos. Your friend will turn up eventually. They always do.'

Love was easy when times were hard. There were moments when Hemingway woke in the morning, before the injuries and aches began to murmur their daily introductions, when he felt as if he would never die. And if not that, then he could no longer care when or how death came to him.

These were the moments when the first thing he would be conscious of was him putting his arm on Martha's naked stomach, her spine pushed against his gut, the backs of her thighs resting on the top of his. He would bring his foot up and tap the sole of hers with the hard top of his, and then he would think to lean in and smell the back of her neck where her skin met her scalp. There was the scent of her hair and the feel of her smooth skin beneath his right hand as he pushed across her midriff, pulling her into him.

He no longer called her 'daughter'. He settled instead on 'Marty'. He never thought to ask her if she liked it.

But it was in those moments that he was sure, somehow, that he and she would never die and that the war might spin on for ever but that they would somehow stay young.

He thought of Pauline and of his sons, then, and the four of them passing through his mind was the signal that he was conscious. He still loved her but in a dimmer way, and he loved them, too, even if it was less vivid than before the war. Before *la causa*.

He had a narrator that might whisper to him in these moments. *You're blowing this, old stick*, it would say. *You are doing the same to her and to them as you did with Hadley and Jack. You're going to blow everything up.*

He missed Jack. He missed Patrick. He missed Greg. He still wanted a daughter.

Sometimes, he thought of the bodies in the warm Florida water, bloated in the heat. He dreamed of them still. But mostly, it was life and death in Spain, and he never had to think about the past. And he never had to think of the future.

All he had to think about was *la causa*. And Marty.

He wondered if they would marry. He wondered if they would have the daughter he wanted. He wondered if she would want to be Mrs Hemingway.

He thought of Dos Passos and of his sad face and grey eyes. He thought of all the seriousness that he was, how he looked too hard at *la causa*, how he looked too hard for the cracks and fractures in *la causa*. How he never enjoyed anything of *la causa* or anything at all, when everything was so serious that all you could do was not take anything seriously at all.

One night, Hemingway and Gellhorn were lying together in the bed, the heat rising from their bodies. It was still cold outside, but they kept the window open. The front line was seventeen blocks away and they could hear the cracks and the pops of the gunfire as the rifles went all night and the machine guns every now and then

blustered out a rally of bangs. Down in the street, a man sang with a hard voice and a trio of drunks argued as they fell and walked along the road.

Hemingway stretched out in the bed, and he felt his toes touch the wood at the end and then he hardened as she put her leg over his.

She whispered into his ear. 'I am very fond of you, Hemingstein.'

They were all at the Hotel Florida. He had seen the photographers Robert Capa and Gerda Taro at breakfast, and Ivens was there, too, and the four of them had that morning seen Errol Flynn drinking in the lobby. Taro had taken a surreptitious photograph of him when she thought he was not looking, but he was, and he turned and smiled at her with yellow teeth so the only thing she could do was grin uneasily back.

Hemingway lay back and closed his eyes. He began to doze into sleep, but there was a high-pitched whine, and he knew what it was before she did. He shook her.

'We need to go.' The whine began to build in volume. It came closer. There were only seconds and then the hotel was hit and the walls shook. 'We need—'

She was already out of the bed, throwing on the grey flannels and a shirt and then she was racing, shoeless and without him, through the door. He rolled out and dressed, following her, and she ran down the corridor towards the stairs.

His knee winced. He felt the ache. *Goddamn it*, the narrator said. *Is this how you want to go? While running?*

They came to the top of the stairs where Antoine de Saint-Exupéry stood, his back stiff, in his pyjamas. He held a wooden bowl filled with grapefruits.

Gellhorn paused.

'We need to get to the shelter, Marty!' Hemingway shouted in her ear.

Saint-Exupéry took one of the grapefruits and offered it to Gellhorn. '*La dame aimerait-elle un pamplemousse?*'

Gellhorn took it. She ran down the stairs in her bare feet. There was another bang, and the walls shook again. The lights blinked off and on. There was a roar of fire. She looked back. She saw Saint-Exupéry with his hand in the bowl, handing a grapefruit to S. B., a war reporter with a black, bobbed hairstyle. Gellhorn heard him say the same thing in French again.

They went into the basement. They cowered with others. They heard the bombs overhead, felt the shake as they landed and the vibrations from their detonation spread across the floor.

Gellhorn's feet were cold on the concrete. She looked around. Everyone in disarray – hair messed up, make-up smeared. She thought, she calculated: all these people, all in each other's bedrooms. Madrid being a hotbed of affairs.

She laughed. She thought of the word 'hotbed'. She laughed again, despite the terror.

Hemingway blinked. He had left his glasses upstairs. 'Marty, what is wrong?' he asked.

'Nothing,' she said. 'Nothing is wrong.' She looked over and saw Dos Passos in a corner, sat by himself with his back to the wall. He looked deep in thought.

The writer Josie Herbst sat in the back of the car with Hemingway. She had taken him outside and into the empty vehicle and closed the door. 'He's dead, Papa,' she said.

'What did you say, daughter?' Hemingway looked at Herbst. She knew everyone. Everyone knew her. Hemingway knew everyone. Everyone knew him.

He looked at her. She was also a writer. They had the same friends. He thought that Marty might end up like her in ten years or so if she developed hope and lost the cynicism. He knew that cynicism was the belief that things would always remain the same. Hope was that they could change.

'He's dead, Papa.'

'Who is?'

'Robles. They killed him.' Herbst lit a cigarette and opened the car window. She inhaled, then breathed the smoke out into the street. 'That's what I hear.'

'From whom?'

'People.'

'Good people?'

'Good people.' She took another, deeper drag and then threw the remaining half-cigarette out into the street. 'I know', she said, 'that they're scarce, but I can live with losing this one.'

'Who killed him?'

'Our side. No one's sure why, but it seems he overheard something with Gorev that he shouldn't have, and it was embarrassing to our dear comrades. So, they killed him to make sure. Took him away from his family and then...' She brought her hand up like a gun and mock-fired it, her fingers pointing down. 'Or maybe he was a traitor?'

'A traitor?'

'Today's patriot can be tomorrow's traitor, without a change in anything.'

'Dos will be devastated.'

'Dos needs to be careful. He's been asking questions for too long. It's better sometimes to know when to stop.'

'Is he in danger?'

'I can't be sure.'

'But you think he is.'

Herbst nodded. 'How do you want to do it?'

*Tell Dos Passos*, the narrator told him. *Tell him so he cannot react. Use that great intellect of his against him. Use it to help him.* Hemingway thought. He calculated angles, approaches. He looked at it like a general.

'There's a luncheon tomorrow with the Russians,' he told Herbst. 'We'll tell him there, at the table, in front of them. He won't react straight away.'

He took Gellhorn to the luncheon. They shook hands with everybody. He went to sit at the top table next to Dos Passos. Dos Passos looked at him. Dos Passos looked through him.

The first course came. Everyone made speeches. He looked at Dos Passos. Dos Passos looked at everyone else. Dos Passos looked at someplace far beyond the room. His eyes were a shade duller than normal. He looked emptied, spent.

The second course came. He ate. Dos Passos picked. Hemingway leaned over. 'Eat, Dos. You need it here.'

Dos Passos looked at him, looked back at his plate.

'Eat, Dos.'

The plates were taken away. The wine was refilled. Hemingway gripped Dos Passos's arm. It felt thin. He leaned over again. He cleared his throat. 'I'm sorry, Dos,' he said. 'They killed him. Your friend Robles. He's been killed.'

Dos Passos stiffened. He turned towards Hemingway. His mouth opened. He knew. He had always known.

'I don't know where he is, Dos, but they took him and they killed him. Don't react now, Dos. Don't react now.'

Dos Passos sat, stared at his plate. He rubbed at his eye, felt the dirt on his finger in the socket. The finger shone when he took it away.

'Let's get you out of here.'

They walked in silence for ten minutes to Plaza Mayor. Hemingway kept his hand on Dos Passos's arm. The air was still cold, though not as sharp as when they had arrived. The crowds on the street stepped around them. Hemingway looked at the soldiers. He had been one of them once. Dos Passos looked at the same soldiers, wondered if it had been one of them who had shot José.

There was the sound of shells landing somewhere, and they stopped for a few seconds. Hemingway looked at Dos Passos. He knew to let him have the air. They looked to where the dry whacking noises of the shells landing had come from, and they could see the yellow smoke in the air.

'Not a good place for tourists, is it?' said Hemingway.

They stepped off the pavement into the street, and Hemingway felt a squelch beneath his foot. He looked down and saw blood that was not his. It was thick and in one place on the ground. Someone had tried to flood it away with hot water, but it had run back into a deep puddle. There was the smell of cordite. 'Too much for one man,' Hemingway said, almost to himself. 'There must have been a few of them.'

At Plaza Mayor, they walked into the centre of the square, far from prying eyes.

'Was he square, Dos? Robles, was he square?'

'Of course he was.'

'Was there any danger he was working for the other side? That's

what I'm hearing. That they thought he was passing information on.'

'No, never.'

'I'm sorry, Dos, but I think you should leave it alone from here on. You know now what happened.'

Dos Passos looked up at his friend. He felt angry, defeated. 'My friend is dead,' he said. There was a shimmer of rage over the flatness of his voice.

'I know, Dos, and you've been a good friend to him, but I think you should leave it alone now. There are things that a man and comrade must do in these difficult and serious war times.'

'Why?'

'It's dangerous here.'

'Who told you that?'

'Josie.'

Dos Passos took off his hat and wrung it in his hands. 'She's an old communist who probably *is* working for them. She would say that.'

'He's still dead, Dos. They no longer trusted him. Don't give them a reason to not trust you. Be smart.'

Dos Passos looked around them, at the near-empty square, the few people in it settling like pigeons. He thought, he calculated. He knew Hemingway was right. He knew there was no trust in their side. He knew there never had been. He thought, he calculated. 'We need to go back home and tell everyone what happened,' he said.

Hemingway shook his head. 'We do that, and the New York reviewers will kill us. They will demolish us for ever. This is a good war for us. For them. For *us*!'

'How can you think like that?'

Hemingway looked down. *Break it*, the narrator told him. *Break him.* 'All I can say, Dos, is that I think the whole thing is a pretty good story and that I *will* write it sometime.'

# 5

# REPUBLIC OF STEEL
# (1936 TO 1937)

The end was coming.

Marc Blitzstein saw it in his wife's hollowed eyes and in her pared-down face. Her hair was thin, too, and her skin was yellow, and her smile was weak as much as it was real.

She now mostly lay in the bed, and he tended to her as much as he could. He dabbed water onto her dry lips when she wanted it, and he held her hand as much as he could, and he held it as long as she wanted him to. He cleaned her. He tried to feed her when she felt that she could not feed herself. He spooned milk into her mouth when she wanted to try. He spooned in just as much as she could taste.

He looked at her in the bed, and it was late, and he assumed that she was sleeping and that she would do so until the morning, so he sat by the low lamp in her room and he wrote down notation.

It was Bertolt Brecht who had told him to expand that little song, the one about the prostitute and the rich man, and now Blitzstein tried to think of what the lives of those characters would have been outside of the borders he had drawn for them. He tapped his fingers

lightly, music without sound, on the wooden arm of the chair for the tempo, and he imagined those same fingers back and forth at the piano, running down the keys and playing the notes and tunes that would come together.

The ideas came. He scratched at the paper with his pencil, the notes for the music in his mind, and he thought about all of the things – on the paper and off – that might come next.

Eva stirred in the bed, and he turned to look over, expecting to see her still asleep, but her eyes were open. She smiled at him over the brown stubs of her teeth.

'Am I being too loud?' he asked. He thought that the scratching of the pencil may have been too much.

'No.'

'Are you OK?'

'No,' she paused. 'Marc, I feel the end is near.'

He loved her. He had always loved her. Tears filled his eyes. 'I know.'

'I'm sorry.'

'It's me that should be sorry.'

She moved her hand and made some space for him on the bed. 'Come and sit with me again,' she said. He still heard it in her voice when she spoke, that rich trace of Berlin that she had never lost. That sliver that reminded him of other times in his life, far from her. He sometimes wondered if it was that German seam in her voice that had brought him to love her.

There was not time enough to think about it now, so Blitzstein got up from the chair and crept to the other side of the room. The floor creaked beneath his feet, and he stepped gingerly towards her in his thick, woollen socks.

'You know,' she said through the thin crack that was now her smile, 'that you cannot wake me if I'm already awake?'

Blitzstein smiled. 'I do this out of habit.'

'And out of love?'

He choked, recovered himself. 'Every time. Always.'

He sat down on the bed, and she held his hand between hers. She caressed it, and she felt his soft skin and his long fingers, the flesh so full and supple. She saw the bones and tendons of hers that moved just beneath the surface of her own, and she saw all the things that should have remained hidden. 'I pushed it too far, I guess.'

'We didn't know.'

'It all stands to reason.' There was no need to say anything else. She felt his hand a little more and then nestled hers in it. 'That feels good,' she said.

'I am sorry,' he said, again, and it was a phrase that she had heard him say so many times before. 'I am sorry.'

'For what?'

'For *it*. But you know I love you, and you know that I would have changed *it* if I could.'

'I know.'

'It's just physical. We are more than that.'

She glowered at him, her thin eyebrows knotting together. 'No, you know better. I was never enough for you, never all you wanted. And I made my peace with all that.'

He put his hand on her thin leg. 'But this.'

'This is nothing to do with it. This is something else.'

'I do love you, Eva.'

'I love you, too, Marc. Now get in and hold me.'

He climbed onto the bed, afraid of hurting her, and he lay down and put his arms around her. He put his chin on the back of her neck. He felt the thinness of her skin beneath the bristles of his beard. He thought about tickling her a little with his moustache

because she had always loved that, but he stopped. 'Is that OK?' he asked.

'Just right.' She closed her eyes and seemed to doze. She wrapped her fingers around his hand. 'Are you still working on that piece?'

'The one about the whore?'

'An ugly word. Say "prostitute" instead.'

'The one about the prostitute. Yes. I think it will be a good piece when it's finished. It may even be a full piece. I'm just working out the story. That's the important piece. Once I have that, the rest will flow.'

'That's good.'

'What will you call it?'

'I thought *Republic of Steel*.'

She shook her head. He heard the rustle of her skin and hair against the pillow. 'Pick something else. Something… gentler. No one wants to see a musical with the word "steel" in it. Get a title that they think they will enjoy. Make it safe.'

'Make it safe?'

'Make them think of something from childhood. A lullaby.'

'How about… *The Rocking of the Cradle*?'

'Almost, but it sounds like a cheap murder novel.' She tightened her hand around his. '*The Cradle Will Rock*. That's it. That's the name. Go with that one.'

'OK. I'll make it *The Cradle Will Rock*.'

'And finish it, won't you?'

'I will.'

'Sing to me, Marc. Words if you have them, notes if you don't. But sing to me. I'd like to hear you sing to me as I fall asleep.'

Weeks after, after she had gone and he had placed her into the earth, Blitzstein went back to the apartment, and he started once again to

write, and he forced himself into what he called a 'white heat' to finish it. A modern opera, different styles, each song moving along the story and the action. And he dedicated himself to it because of her. He thought that to think so deeply about her might take him to a place that he could not return from. And six weeks later, his nerves and his energy almost spent, he took an invite to the apartment of Orson and Virginia Welles, where he played the whole thing, him doing all the roles, on a piano that was a half-step away from needing desperately to be retuned.

It was a few days later in the back office of the Maxine Elliott's Theatre, and Orson Welles had a glint in his eye. A smile curled like a waning moon across his face. It was not a sneer, more the grin of someone about to give a gift more for themselves than for the receiver. He tapped on the door of John Houseman's office and, without waiting, stepped in.

Inside, Houseman looked up at the door Welles had just come in through. 'One day,' he said, in his clipped accent that he was always sure to make sure people knew was English, not British, 'you are going to come in and I'll not be here but out somewhere else doing something that will surprise you.'

'I'm sure, House,' Welles replied, 'that if you were going to surprise me, you would have to be in the same room as I am to do it.'

Houseman smiled. 'What do you want, Orson?'

Welles smiled back. 'What makes you think that I want something?'

'You never come in here unless there's something – one more chorister, a new lighting man, some more time for a rewrite. It's an ongoing theme. Remember when you first asked me to do the voodoo version of *Macbeth*? I do; it was in this room.' He motioned around him.

Welles took off his overcoat and moved to the chair in front of Houseman's desk. 'Well…'

'I knew it. You wouldn't be sitting down unless it was something big.'

Welles took a cigar from his pocket and lit it. Acrid smoke came from his mouth in little puffs as the tobacco took light. There was an immediate shift in the air in the small room. 'I have something big. Our next project.'

'Another project?'

'Indeed.' He reached down and picked up his briefcase, opened it and placed a thick sheaf of paper onto Houseman's desk. The Englishman looked down at it. 'We did *Horse Eats Hat*, and then the composer came to a party at mine and Virginia's,' said Welles, 'and he played this whole thing for us. It was remarkable.'

'It was remarkable that you were with Virginia. I don't know how it is that you two stay together; you're never there.'

'That is the secret to a successful marriage: not being there.' Welles tapped the paper again. 'Read it,' he said.

Houseman looked down. *The Cradle Will Rock*. 'And this is?'

'Our next production. A big musical. It'll bring people in from all around, and they will love us for it.'

'That sounds spectacular.'

'It will be.' Welles dragged out the last word for a split-second longer. 'But it will be expensive.'

'Ah, there it is.'

'Read the book, and then we'll take it to Flanagan, and see what she says.'

Houseman had, a few hours later, read the play. He went out into the seats of the theatre where he and Welles were running Project

891, the arts division of the Federal Theatre Project, and sat in the row behind the young director.

'You've seen what's going on, haven't you?'

Welles leaned his head back. He raised his eyebrows. 'No?'

'Everyone is so scared of communists and communism that all we ever do is walk on eggshells, and now you bring us this pro-union, eat-the-rich masterpiece and expect us to put it on.'

'So it's a masterpiece?'

'Yes, damn it. That doesn't mean it's good for us.' Houseman glowered at him. He read the look on the young man's face. 'You know exactly what you're doing, Orson. There's no way that Flanagan is going to sign off on this. You must be mad.'

Welles smiled. 'That's exactly what I want, House. I want her to *not* do it, so we can go off and do it ourselves. No more government, no more Federal Theatre Project. We will be such pariahs that we'll have all the freedom to do whatever it is that we want to do.'

'What *you* want to do.'

Welles shrugged, nodded his head from side to side. 'That's an academic difference.'

'It's not, Orson. It's really not.'

'So are we doing it?'

'*The Cradle Will Rock*?'

'Yes. Are we taking it to Flanagan?'

'Yes, damn it. But this is your baby, not mine.'

Hallie Flanagan sat in her office in New York, the script for *The Cradle Will Rock* on the wooden desk in front of her. She was forty-six years old and had been running the Federal Theatre Project, which fell under the auspices of the Works Progress Administration, for two years. All of it had been set up by President Roosevelt

to boost the economy in the fallout of the Great Depression, and so Flanagan spent her days like a fireman, running from one blaze to another, trying to put each one out before hurtling off again.

She was tired, but she was energised. She loved theatre and always had, and she saw goodness in all those who worked for her, and she carried the weight of their employment on her narrow shoulders, knowing that a cut in funding in one place or another would mean the loss of hundreds, maybe thousands, of jobs.

And most of Washington hated the Federal Theatre Project, seeing it as too left wing, subversive to an America that they claimed as their own. And so when she was not managing the egos and tantrums of thousands of artists, she was alternately applying fire, then balms, to the egos and tantrums of career politicians looking to see which way the crowd wanted them to go, then following it.

And now she had Welles, this terrible child of the New York stage, and his new project. She had been with him as he did play after play, each one an amazement, and she could see how extraordinary he was even if she wondered how he would ever survive outside the microcosm of the Federal Theatre Project.

Flanagan tapped her finger on the bound papers in front of her and pursed her lips. She was a small woman with short, tight hair, and she had a way to glance briefly at someone with a wither that made them take a full step back. She gave a short, snorting exhale, cocked her head and gave the two men in front of her a blast of wither so full that it bordered on contempt.

'You know the battles I fight, right, Orson? There are 18 million people unemployed in this country, and I am trying to not add a few thousand more to that.'

A little smile from the boy. 'I do,' he said. The small hitch in his mouth remained in place. 'I think this is exemplary.'

Flanagan nodded. 'And of everything, this is the one you bring to me? This one? And how much do you think it will cost to put on at the Maxine Elliott?'

Houseman looked at Welles, then at Flanagan. 'We've done some initial calculations,' he said, his voice more clipped than usual. Flanagan thought she could detect a smile in his face, too.

'Go on.'

Welles took out a cigar. 'Well,' he said, as he struck a match and lifted it to his face.

'Don't,' said Flanagan. 'Not in here.'

Welles moved the match away. 'Very well,' he said. 'We think we could do it for $100,000.'

Flanagan blinked. '$100,000?'

'Around that.'

She leaned back in her chair, looked out of her window at the bustling streets below and made a smacking, pursing noise with her lips. 'One. Hundred. Thousand,' she said, dropping each word out like a farmer seeding his land. Each word seemed to come fully formed into the air, then faded to nothing, replaced at its end by the next one.

'It's a lot,' said Houseman, apologetically. There was an underlying confidence that began to fill the emptiness in his voice.

'It is.' Flanagan stood up and walked slowly to the cabinet in her office. She opened the door slightly and debated whether it was too early for a stiff drink or even too late. 'So you want me to use $100,000 of my meagre resources to bankroll *The Cradle Will Rock*?'

'That's right,' said Welles.

'This is an opera—'

'We thought,' said Welles, 'that we could do it like a musical.'

'A *musical*. I'm sorry. You want me to use $100,000 of my meagre

resources to do a musical? And this musical starts with a prostitute who has been stiffed by the local steel magnate who runs Steeltown USA and has been arrested for kicking up a stink, rightfully, about it. And in the prison cell, she meets all the people – the union leader, the minister, the newspaperman – who have also all fallen afoul of this magnate. And then they begin to sing about the benefits and intrinsic good of being part of a union? And you want me to do all this with Washington on my back at every turn about the left-wing bias – and, yes, we have some of that because we are theatre people, damn it – of the Federal Theatre Project?'

Welles smiled. He looked at Houseman. Houseman smiled back. 'That's correct,' they said together.

Flanagan nodded. 'OK. Well, I love it. Just bring me the receipts.'

They began work on the production. They bought costumes and built sets. They assembled singers and dancers. The costs went up. The production got bigger. It got more elaborate.

*We'll make it into a musical like the others*, thought Welles. *They'll see the poster, and we'll grab them by the eyes. And then they'll sit, and we will grab them by the heart!*

Washington noticed. Washington did not like *The Cradle Will Rock*. Word came down to Flanagan: *Drop the show*. She held fast. More words came down: *Your left-wing bias will be your downfall. Be smart*. She held fast. The President was looking at re-election, said he could not help her. She held fast. Congress protested. She held fast.

On 27 May, as cuts loomed on the horizon, 7,000 of the 9,000 people working for the Works Progress Administration walked out of work. They cited the unseen cuts moving towards them.

Flanagan held fast.

She smiled when she had to. She pushed back gently. She held her breath, and she hoped Welles and Houseman would pull it off.

The summer began to come. The heat began to rise. She read the *New York Times*. She read about Spain. She read about the left and the right fighting for the soul of another country. She knew the death of the Federal Theatre Project meant the death of 9,000 jobs. People were hot. People were angry. Eight years since the Great Depression. Tensions in Europe meant that America might get involved. America might not.

Agitation abroad. Agitation at home. *This is a great country*, she thought, *when we choose to be.*

She sat each night in her apartment in the silence, the world a few moves away. She loved the silence. She rested in it. She voiced things in her head in her private moments, the thoughts an affirmation.

One night, she sat in front of a mirror and she saw her tired eyes and her tired skin. She pressed her fingers against her eyelids.

She muttered to herself: 'This cradle *will* rock.'

She held fast.


It was the end of May, two weeks before *The Cradle Will Rock* was set to open, and the weather on the south side of Chicago was warm and pleasant. There were families there, and the crowd had assembled at a former dance hall named Sam's Place, and they had come dressed in their best clothes, the atmosphere convivial, and they were to march peacefully in support of a union for the workers at Republic Steel, who had been on strike for a week.

There was about 2,000 of them and they were walking so that Republic, one of the smaller steelmakers, would recognise the union. The law had given them the right two years before to organise and strike peacefully.

The writer Howard Fast would remember that Memorial Day as one for picnics and boating or a trip to the beach. It was, he wrote later for *New Masses*, 'a day when patriotic sentiments could be washed down comfortably with Coca-Cola or a Tom Collins, as you preferred'. Fast was there, walking amongst the crowds alongside the reporter and writer Dorothy Day.

A few hundred yards away were the police, hot in their blue woollen uniforms, and they looked across that distance at the crowd, and they felt the weight of their weapons on their belts and in their tunics. It was Republic that had armed them from its stockpile of clubs and guns and which had given them the teargas. And it was Republic that did not want the strike, that wanted it all to end so that things could return to the way they had been before.

There was a camera crew there, too, shooting newsreel for Paramount, and they were watching the crowd and the police, and it seemed that everyone was watching everyone else.

The crowd began to move, all 2,000 of them, walking across the prairie not far from the border between Illinois and Indiana, and they walked up to the 200 police in their hot uniforms, and they locked arms with each other and stopped some fifty yards away.

One of the policemen called out. 'Who are you? Are you union?'

The crowd remained silent. A slight wind came across the prairie and cooled everything and everyone for a few seconds. It was as if the only sounds to be heard were that of the breathing of warm air and the beating of over 2,000 hearts.

The policeman called out again. 'Who are you? Are you union?'

A small voice piped up from the crowd, a few people back from the front. 'I'm union!'

The focus of every policeman was on the voice, and they looked for its speaker. Another deeper voice called out. 'I'm union.'

'I'm also union!'

'And me!'

Now, a feminine voice and it was mocking. 'Hell, I'm union, too!'

The crowd began to laugh. 'Hey,' someone called, 'I think he's union over there!'

'I'm union!'

The snickers began to build. The laughter continued.

'Don't look at me. I'm not union!' A pause, a laugh. 'OK, I'm union!'

Laughter rolled from the crowd and into the police. The word 'union' echoed around the prairie.

A policeman stepped forward. Then another. A pall began to drop. There was a stillness in the air like a caught breath.

The police charged, batons out. The crowd turned, too slowly, to flee, and the batons came down on their backs and their shoulders. They tried to run. A man in the mass of people fell and then he was trampled, and then others started falling to the ground as the teargas canisters began to hiss and billow.

It was chaos now, and families fled away from the police, and the batons continued to come down not only on shoulders and backs and heads but on the legs of everyone who had fallen, and the police continued.

There was a gunshot, and someone in the crowd fell. And then there was another. The police began firing at everyone now, bullets hitting backs, the victims falling. The crowd kept running, beginning to scatter. But still the bullets came.

There were wagons and the police began to pick people from the crowd and drag them away. They put them in the vans, blood thick on the floor, and when the vehicles were overfilled, a hard hand would smack against the side and then they would lurch off across the grass.

The cameras whirred. They caught everything. Four bodies lay on the floor. Six more would die later. Twenty-four others went to hospital. A further eighty were wounded.

Paramount had the footage. They held it back. They were fearful of 'inciting riots'. They recut and released it, made the strikers into the villains. They praised the police. The status quo held fast.

A closed Senate committee was formed. They got the film from Paramount. Paramount said it had not been edited. Paramount lied. It was still enough to outrage the committee.

It was Flanagan who took the call from Washington on 10 June, days before *The Cradle Will Rock* was set to open. She listened, nodded silently, put the phone down and sat quietly at her desk for a few moments. Then, she began to make other calls, write memos and let people know that the budget was to be cut by nearly a third.

Eventually, she called the Maxine Elliott's Theatre, where Welles and Houseman were, and she told them the news. Welles was uncharacteristically silent.

'What does this mean', he said, eventually, 'for the show?'

'It's off, Orson.'

'We've sold 18,000 tickets for the run. The show is ready. And it's bad for everyone, and for it, if it does not open.'

'It's not going to happen. They're saying that no play is to open before 1 July.'

Welles was angry. She could hear it rise in his throat to meet his words. 'This will kill us.'

Flanagan began to weep. 'I know.'

Afterwards, Welles and Houseman sat together in the empty theatre bar. Welles looked over at Houseman and smiled.

'Well...' he said, then he stopped. The smile crept into being something self-assured. 'Well,' he said, again.

Houseman looked at him. 'Well, what?'

'Well, I guess we put on the dress rehearsal. We don't actually have to open just yet.'

'If we open at all.'

There was that smile from Welles again.

They did the final dress rehearsal four days later. There were missed cues, and the cast still struggled with the music. The musicians seemed rusty. Everything was not quite there.

Behind the stage, watching from the wings, Welles began to sweat in the June heat. He took off his jacket and loosened his shirt collar, and he thought of all the things that were not working.

He thought of Flanagan, who he knew suspected him and Project 891. And he thought of how she knew he was planning something but was purposefully looking in a different direction, explaining over her shoulder and from one side of her mouth to Washington that it was something to do with artists and fulfilling their contracts and that, no, the show would not be opening.

Welles leaned forward, and he saw the half-full theatre, every person in its stalls knowing that the show was not going to open. And he thought for a second that maybe it was right that they should not and that it was too much and at the wrong time.

The rehearsal finished, and the cast walked out onto the stage. He felt someone grip his arm and he looked down and saw Houseman, and he whispered, 'What?'

Houseman nodded and led him out onto the stage, under the bright lights.

The crowd stood and all of them cheered, and Welles stood,

blinking, and he thought, *This is not right. We were not good enough today for this.*

He looked at Houseman. Houseman looked back. 'They know it's something bigger than them, Orson. Something bigger than us.'

The play was to open two days later, on 16 June, and when Welles and Houseman arrived at the theatre doors, they found them padlocked with federal guards stood outside.

'What is this?' asked Welles of one of them.

The guard tapped a sign, new and now hanging on the door: NO SHOW TONIGHT.

Welles snorted. 'I can read that, dear boy,' he said, 'but what is going on? Why are you here?'

The guard looked at Welles, and he shrugged apologetically. 'I've just been sent here,' he said and pointed to his colleague, 'along with him, to make sure that nobody takes any government property from here.'

Welles flared his nostrils. '*Any government property?*' he asked.

'Yes, sir.'

Welles looked at the guard's uniform, the collar too tight around his neck. He saw the sweat in the man's brow and the fullness of the brown in his eyes that seemed filled with shame. He reached out and put his hand on his arm. 'Very well,' he said, as softly as he could muster in his anger. 'Very well.' He turned and his shoulders slumped a little, and he moved to walk down West 39th Street and towards 6th Avenue, the New York traffic and its people around him unaware of what was happening.

'Mr Welles, I am sorry, but the government has told me.'

Welles turned. He was surprised the man knew him. He saw that he was someone who might have come to see one of his plays and

who may have seen his picture in the paper. He saw, in him doing the job, that he was doing it to feed others – a wife and, maybe, children. 'I know,' Welles said, 'but tell me, what does the government count as its property?'

'The costumes, the scenery. Anything like that.'

'The play itself?'

The man took off his hat and rubbed at the bald spot on his head, and he looked down. 'I guess not.'

Welles nodded and clicked his tongue.

Somehow, Welles snuck into the offices at the back of the theatre where Houseman soon joined him. The two began to plot.

'Let's find a new theatre,' Welles said. 'Tonight. We'll open there.'

Houseman clicked his tongue, loosened his tie. He ran the idea through his head. He thought about it. 'The sets? The costumes?'

'We won't need them.'

'That's a lot of work for something that we don't need.'

Archie MacLeish and lighting whizz Jean Rosenthal came into the office. 'What's going on?' MacLeish said.

Houseman swivelled in his chair. 'We're going to find somewhere to put the show on tonight. A new theatre. And we're going to do it *sans* costumes and scenery. Just the cast, if we have to.'

'Are you sure?'

'Never ask me if I'm sure!' shouted Welles. 'They've padlocked the front door! That is the final insult!'

MacLeish sat down on the edge of Houseman's desk. 'Our big musical number, that you've spent weeks rehearsing, getting everyone to work together on cue and in time with one another, we're going to move the whole thing to a new theatre – which we haven't found yet – and perform with just one piano?'

Houseman lit a cigarette. His fingers shook. 'Yes, that's what Orson and I were thinking—'

'Yes.' Welles's voice boomed in the room, a strong chord struck in the middle of an overture that brought everything bracingly to a stop. 'Yes.'

MacLeish, Rosenthal and Houseman looked at Welles. He looked, in turn, at each one of them and said in a voice that left no room for debate, 'We are going to do this.'

MacLeish looked at him. 'Orson, they will crucify you.'

Welles swivelled his head. The jocularity they were used to had disappeared and it seemed that they had come to the hard wood deep inside the young artist they considered a genius. 'The government is shutting this down and it is censorship by another name,' Welles said. 'It comes politely and asks for answers it ignores for questions it has already made up its mind about. And it hates *The Cradle Will Rock* and all the politics of it, and it will do anything it can to stop us while still holding a smile on its face.'

Houseman pointed to Welles, spoke to MacLeish and Rosenthal. 'He's serious.'

'You're right, I'm serious!' thundered Welles. His voice rose like a storm whipping itself into its most destructive form. 'We are talking about the problems that we have here in this country and problems that every politician, in Washington or not, is seeking to ignore. They'll ignore these problems here in America, and they have been ignoring these problems in Spain. The problem is freedom. Freedom of expression, freedom of the soul.'

Welles straightened up and walked to the window. He looked out of it onto the street, at the faces of people walking outside, and he pointed unseen to them. 'So long as these problems are not solved,'

he said, 'so long as ignorance and poverty remain on earth, these words cannot be useless!'

He crossed back across the office, walking around the desk and went to his overcoat, from which he removed his billfold. He took ten dollars from it and handed it to Rosenthal. 'Find a piano and a driver,' he said, 'and drive around the city. Call us every ten minutes while we look for a theatre. If... *when* we find one, we'll tell you where to go.'

After Rosenthal left the room, MacLeish excused himself so he could find a telephone in another part of the theatre. Once the pair had gone, Houseman turned and put his hand on Welles's arm. '*These words cannot be useless*,' he repeated back to him. 'You've had that phrase in your head for a while, haven't you?'

Welles smiled. 'It's for that *Les Misérables* I've been working on.'

'And did you write them?'

Welles smiled once more.

Welles, Houseman and MacLeish began to call around. Each theatre was booked or closed or could not for one reason or another be used. Rosenthal called every ten minutes. They could hear the click and the hiss of the lines being tapped at the theatre.

'Good evening, politicians,' Welles said to whoever was listening in. 'Welcome to *The Orson Welles Show*, live for you right now from the Maxine Elliott's Theatre in New York City, New York, USA! Now, as you will hear, I'm about to call our lawyer.'

He got the lawyer Arnold Weissberger on the phone. Weissberger told him to find a theatre without a federal lease. 'They can't touch you after that,' he said.

'Thank you.' Welles went to put down the phone.

'But, Orson…'

'What?'

'Your orchestra musicians are with the union. They won't be allowed to play in any theatre that's not a federal one without full Broadway salaries. That's a higher rate not just for tonight but for at least two weeks of rehearsals.'

They called more places. More dead ends: closed. Too much money. Union houses, meaning they would be forced to pay the cast more, with more paid rehearsal time, impossible at late notice and for the Federal Theatre Project.

Rosenthal called. 'I've got a piano,' she said. 'It's not great, from some bar near Times Square. It's $10, and another $5 for the driver.'

'Do it,' said Welles.

Welles put down the phone. It rang again. A local school of music was calling to ask if the show was going to open.

'Of course it is!' cried Welles. 'We don't know where yet! But it will open!'

At 4 p.m., with no theatre, Rosenthal called again. 'The driver has said he's only giving us one more hour,' she said.

'OK,' Welles said, quietly, over the phone. 'Keep going, as long as you can. Keep calling. We'll keep trying.'

Eventually, they left the Maxine Elliott, sneaking past the guards, and went to the bar on the corner where they ordered shots of whiskey. A small old man sat next to them, his head staring down at the wood of the bar. Welles clapped him on the shoulder. 'A glass, friend?'

The old man looked up at him. 'Sure. Thank you.'

'You're welcome.' Welles clapped his hand to his broad chest, then looked to Houseman. 'House, I've left my billfold at the theatre. Can you…' He motioned to the bar.

Houseman sighed. 'Yes, I've got it, Orson.'

They sat in a line at the bar, and they stared at their drinks. 'I guess this may be it,' MacLeish said, more to himself than anyone else. He held his glass between two fingers, tipped it one way and then the other. The brown liquid rocked from side to side. 'I guess there really was nothing we could do.'

Welles glowered. 'I guess so,' he said. 'I guess it's back to repertory. You have any ideas, House?'

Houseman shook his head. 'The Comedy?'

Welles shook his head. 'We can't use a union house. They won't touch us.'

MacLeish spoke. 'And 49th Street is the same.'

Welles fingered his glass. 'The Empire is derelict. They're repainting the Guild.'

Houseman sighed. 'The National.'

'Too expensive,' said Welles. 'I guess, well, it's all a bit hopeless.'

The three lapsed into silence.

The old small man beside them in the dark suit spoke. 'Why don't,' he suggested, stammering, 'why don't you just take my theatre?'

Welles put down his glass and turned on his stool. 'You have a theatre?'

The old man nodded. 'I do. I'm the booking agent. We're free tonight.'

'Where is it?'

'The Venice on 932 Seventh.'

'How many seats?'

'About 1,700.'

Welles looked at Houseman. 'That's three times what we can hold.'

'They can bring friends. We'll give tickets away. For every one bought, we'll give them another two.'

Welles took hold of the small man in the dark suit's shoulder again. 'Tell me,' he asked. 'How much?'

'Let's say $100?'

Welles looked at Houseman. 'Can we do that? Can *you* do that?'

Houseman smiled, and it was a smile that started small but grew big. His voice lost some of its clipped-down timbre. 'Of course I can, Orson,' he shouted. 'Of course I can!'

'We have a plan,' Welles said, clearing his throat. He and Houseman gathered the play's actors in the stalls of the Maxine Elliott. They sat together, impossibly small against the backdrop of nearly 600 empty seats. It was late afternoon, and the heat was building, but the stage lights had been turned on completely.

Olive Stanton was in the second row. She was the lead in the play, and for her the Federal Theatre Project had been a lifeline, some way to earn money when things were so bad. She had been with the play from the start, had seen the effects of the politicians on Welles and Houseman and now she was confused and troubled because she did not know what she was supposed to do, with the play no longer opening.

Welles went silent, and he looked down between his feet at the thin carpet. He stood with his back against the stage, and then he looked up at all of them with a glint in his eye.

'We have a plan,' he said, again. Looking from one performer to the next, he said, 'The government has decreed that we are not to open *The Cradle Will Rock* tonight. That is its decision, although it has not been honest enough to come out and state that as a fact. Instead, they have decided that we are to endure the budget cuts by not opening as planned. Their hope is that we will not open at all. And that is their decision. But everything behind me,' he said,

and with this he swept his arm over the elaborate sets, towards the costumes hung like carcasses, 'belongs to the government.'

He straightened up, pulled at his shirt cuffs. 'However, we are not property of the government. We are free agents and performers. And we can do whatever we want and wherever we want. Just not with government property.'

Welles was warmed up now. 'We will be going to the Venice Theatre with Marc, tonight. And he is going to be performing, on piano, *The Cradle Will Rock*. He may even do some of the parts himself, although I would hope he does not.' A smile. 'If you all were there, sat in those seats, there is nothing to stop you as US citizens from standing, I believe, and speaking your parts from those seats when your cue comes.'

Welles looked over to Houseman, who sat in the darkness in the second seat. 'That's right, Orson,' Houseman said.

'Thank you, House.'

The performers looked between themselves. They murmured. Olive Stanton looked at Welles, and she smiled.

'Now, if you excuse me,' said Welles. 'We have a paying public outside and I need to tell them where to go! A full house, ladies and gentlemen! Bring your friends! Two tickets free for every one bought!'

Welles went from the stage door of the theatre and jogged around the building to see a few hundred people stood outside the Maxine Elliott, waiting to get in. The guards were still there. He stopped and mopped his brow, then walked to the front of the queue, stopping every few feet to say something and announce his presence.

When he reached the locked doors, he stopped and with a dramatic flourish, reached down and took hold of the padlock, then let it swing against the wood. There was a *thunk* from the impact.

The crowd watched him. He cleared his throat.

'Ladies and gentlemen,' he said, speaking over the heads of those in front and aiming his words at the back. He took a long, deep breath. 'Ladies and gentlemen, I want to apologise personally for your ordeal, of having to wait in the heat outside of a locked door. And I'm afraid that I am going to have to ask you for a little more.'

There was some murmured chatter in the crowd. One or two people took a sideways step so that they could see him better.

'Ladies and gentlemen,' Welles continued, 'we are going to do something that we have not seen in more than two millennia of theatre performances. As you can see to the side of me, the federal government has shut down this production. It is, the government says, too dangerous for your eyes to see and your ears to hear. But despair not!'

He began to pace down the line, and heads turned to follow him. 'What we are going to do is go that way!' He pointed north, towards Central Park. 'We are not only going to shift this production but to move with it its entire audience. That is—' He spun and pointed to each of them. '*You!*'

Welles put his hands in front of him and paused. He pushed his palms towards the ground like a magician who has made reappear the rabbit. 'Now, it's twenty blocks in this heat and, once again, I do apologise, but I am asking you to make this journey – call it a pilgrimage – to the Venice Theatre between 58th and 59th on Seventh Avenue. And bring friends – two tickets for every ticket sold!'

He raised a finger to the air. 'You may, of course,' he said, 'ask for a refund and our box office will indeed give you one when they can.' He went back to the door and flicked the lock a second time. A hard *thunk*. 'However, I cannot guarantee when this will – or even if it does – happen.'

With a final flourish, he turned to Houseman who had crept up unseen beside him, took his arm in his and began to walk.

Houseman and Welles walked in the heat, and they occasionally looked behind them. People began to follow them in clumps, walking through Manhattan. Welles and Houseman remained arm in arm.

'You know,' said Houseman, 'it seems that you can make the people do almost anything that you tell them. How do you do it?'

'Magic, my dear House. It's just magic. The thing about magic is that you cannot be a realist if you don't believe in it.'

'Orson, you talk so much.'

Welles squeezed Houseman's arm. 'House, it's all about timing. One time, I went to a party and thought before I left my home that I would do some magic tricks when I got there. So I had a rabbit hidden in my coat and I got there, and I waited and I waited and I waited. And, then, suddenly everyone was leaving, and I got to my car and put my hand in my pocket and realised the rabbit was still there, only now she was asleep, the lining of my pocket was chewed and she had pissed all over me.'

'What are you talking about, Orson?'

'The trick, dear House – the secret of magic – that I learned that evening was that the great magicians know when to take the rabbit out of the pocket!'

Marc Blitzstein stood behind the wings of the Venice Theatre, waiting to go on. The stage was bare, except for the piano, and he could see from the curtains that its wood was scuffed and the upholstery on its seat had begun to fray. He put his hand inside his shirt and felt the rapid beat of his heart. He thought of Eva.

The stalls, he knew, were about two-thirds full, and he waited in the heat by the heavy curtain until his cue to come on.

Moments dropped away, then the lights in the auditorium began to dim and fall. There was a loud clunk as a single spotlight came on and was centred on the piano. His cue.

Blitzstein took a large, dry breath and walked out onto the stage. He stopped halfway between the wing and the piano, nodded to the audience, then sat.

A door opened at the back and Welles and Houseman entered, arm in arm, with the lights from the foyer casting them into silhouette. The single spotlight was swung away from Blitzstein and towards them.

Welles began to walk down the central aisle, leaving Houseman behind.

'Ladies and gentlemen,' he said, 'thank you for coming tonight. Our production, the one you went to see twenty blocks away, is no more. Tonight will not be that production. That production of *The Cradle Will Rock* was a full Broadway musical, with costumes and a full orchestra and dancers. And there was a cast.'

Welles stopped at the bottom of the stage. 'This is as far as we can go,' he said. 'Our musicians and our actors are not allowed on this stage. They cannot play on any other stage than the one they were supposed tonight to play upon. So Mr Blitzstein is going to play his music, himself, on a single piano that we have purloined from some honky-tonk joint, and we hope that you appreciate our efforts.'

Welles looked down. He closed his eyes and pursed his lips. He raised a single finger into the air. 'However, should any of my cast be here in attendance tonight and wish, on cue, to sing their parts as meant, there is no forbidding of that as long as they do not attempt to set foot upon this stage.' There was a wicked smile upon his face,

as softly as he could boom to the auditorium. 'Now, ladies and gentlemen, *The Cradle Will Rock*.'

The light swung back towards Blitzstein. 'Scene one. Street corner,
Steeltown USA,' he said.

He pressed down gently on the piano's keys, and the music began
to fill the auditorium's empty silence.

Blitzstein opened his mouth to sing.

Olive Stanton, in the third row, stood and began her part. The
crowd looked in the darkness in her direction, then the light swung
towards her. There was a long, hard cheer.

Afterwards, after the cast had sung and acted their parts from
across the auditorium, never once standing on stage, Welles and
Houseman took once again to the front. The applause rolled down
from the balcony and along the aisles, and it crashed into them as
a wall of noise.

They smiled. None of it had been for nothing. It had all been for
something.

Houseman squeezed Welles's arm. 'The cradle rocked, Orson,' he
said.

Welles looked down. There was a wetness alongside the sparkle
in his eye. 'That's a terrible line, House,' he said, smiling. 'You should
leave the writing to me.'

The day after *The Cradle Will Rock* opened, Welles and Flanagan
saw each other in Washington. She had asked him to go with her to
speak to the government, but he had chosen to go by himself and
plead his case and Houseman's.

There was a lot of mess, Flanagan realised, and Welles had little
interest in helping to clear or clean any of it. A cradle had been

rocked, and the fallout for the Federal Theatre Project was going to be severe. Cuts, certainly. Annihilation, probably. Jobs lost, either way.

After pleading their cases unsuccessfully and Flanagan attempting to staunch the bleeding wound that was the Federal Theatre Project's future, the two of them took the same late train back to New York. After it left Washington, Flanagan went down its carriages, looking in each one for Welles.

She found him, eventually, and she sat down in the compartment, empty but for the two of them. It was dark outside, and the train rocked a little. Neither of them spoke for the longest time.

It was two days after the showing at the Venice, and *The Cradle Will Rock* was running for another two weeks, but it had become clear that Welles and Houseman were leaving the Federal Theatre Project. The call came from Washington and Houseman was sacked, and Welles had thought for only a second or two before he walked out in solidarity.

Flanagan looked at Welles and she saw the youthful face, the self-satisfaction with what he had done. And she saw fear, too, and it was that of a boy who had defied his father with some daring stunt that had worked out well and gained him applause. She saw, then, that that moment was probably the last in his lifetime that Welles would be a boy, fully, and that he was now a man. Or, at least, on the verge of becoming irreversibly one.

Welles lit a cigar. The rich, dark smell of the burning tobacco began to fill the compartment.

'Tell me,' said Welles. 'What happens now?'

'Nothing good, Orson. Nothing good.'

Welles looked out of the window. 'We had to do it, Hallie,' he said. 'We had a whole show and we had to show the government and

those politicians that would have shut us down what it was that we were willing to do. We had to show them.'

'Oh, you showed them, Orson. And now you'll be off to Hollywood. But you have so much about this wrong. It's not about you.'

Welles looked at her through the dark-blue smoke. He drew on the cigar and it lit up in red, amber-like flames at the end. Some of the tobacco came loose and fluttered towards the floor. 'It never was,' he said.

Flanagan shook her head. 'It was, Orson. It was. It was always about you. Even doing things for other people was just something that made you feel good about yourself. But it was always you, and it always will be in the end.'

'That's just your opinion.'

'It is. But I feel it's one that many are going to hold about you. You're gone now, as is Houseman, but I'm going to be cleaning this up for some time. That's if I can clean it up.'

'The project was dying, anyway.'

The already-dim light above them dimmed a little more, and it looked to Flanagan as if Welles were fading away into the smoke that hung in the air. To him, she was also beginning to fade.

'The thing you've never cared about, Orson,' Flanagan said, 'or understood or ever taken the trouble to find out, is that this is a big country. The Federal Theatre Project is bigger than any production within it. It includes not only *The Cradle Will Rock* but the theatre for the children of coal miners in Gary, Indiana; the enterprise for vaudevillians in Portland, Oregon; the Negro Theatre in Chicago; the research being done in Oklahoma. What do you care for any of these?'

Welles and Houseman went back to the Maxine Elliott for a final time, where they took the last of the things they wanted to take with

them. Houseman had been fired, of course, and now Welles was out of a job, although he was making over $1,500 a week from performing on the radio. Other things were in front of them, although they were still to pick a direction.

They looked again at the lock on the door, and Welles gave it one last rattle for good luck. Then, before Houseman could say anything, Welles hooked his arm in his and spun him around in the street, then began walking them away into Manhattan.

It was not the start of a romance; they do not take as much time. But it was the start of something, even if it was subdued and there was fear and trepidation. But mixed in there was excitement, and it meant that they were free now of the Federal Theatre Project, of its politics and even of Flanagan, whom they both loved and respected deeply.

They walked in silence for a few seconds, arm in arm, and they ignored the looks of the people that passed them by. And when they knew instinctively that they had put enough distance between them and the Maxine Eliott, Houseman turned to Welles and raised his eyebrows. 'And next?' he asked.

'Well,' thought Welles, looking ahead to the horizon, 'well, why don't we go and start our own theatre?'

'Yes,' said Houseman, in a voice subdued because the matter was already decided. 'Yes, we should do that.'

# 6

# NARRATION (1937)

The ambulance whipped through Manhattan, belching smoke and careering from one lane to another, then back again. It shot south through the city as if the devil himself was chasing it. It was insufferably stuffy inside but to open up the windows was then to breathe in the dirty air that was heavy with lead and exhaust fumes that had baked for weeks in the unrelenting heat. The driver pushed his foot down onto the pedal as he came up the intersection of East 12th Street and 5th Avenue, then eased off as he turned, before pushing down once more.

Some sirens blared, and the passenger in the back rolled and rocked against the door, then slid a few inches along the seat. His stomach, which was always bad, roiled and fizzed. He looked out and saw the hot and dry air rise in shimmers from the pavement.

Today was more than just another one in the studio, and this was why they were hurrying, although they were always hurrying from one place to another, from this show to that show to this rehearsal to that party. Such relentless, unstoppable movement had been a fact of their lives for some time.

Up in front, the driver braked, and the wheels skidded on the

asphalt. In the back, Orson Welles put his hands together and offered up a small prayer that the threadbare tyres would continue to hold.

'Let's get this beast there in one piece!' he said to the driver. 'That's the most important thing. I can talk, even with a broken leg. But we must get to this place on time!'

The truth was that a minute or two's lateness would have no impact; it was not a live broadcast, going out to the nation, but it was the chance for Welles to meet *him* – Hemingway, the most famous writer in the world – and Welles did not want the meeting to start in a rough place. After six months of covering the war in Spain, he assumed that Hemingway and his clan would not be in the mood for more conflict.

'I can slow down,' the driver said.

'That would be much preferable to us not getting there,' replied Welles, 'but not by much.'

They continued to zip through the city, the hazy yellow air and the heat thousands of miles from Spain. They swung out again into another lane, overtook a car and then merged back in. A pothole in the road threw Welles two inches into the air from his seat, and he looked ahead and saw a line of vehicles stopped fifty or so yards in front of them.

'Maybe we should use the siren?' he suggested to the driver.

'We can do that.' The siren was switched on, and its drone began to fill the inside of the ambulance. The cars and taxis ahead began to move to the side, with just enough space so that Welles and the driver did not have to slow, slipping through the gaps between them and then speeding up once more.

The ambulance was a trick he had picked up when doing the live radio shows, five or six of them a day, and having to race through Midtown from CBS to NBC, then back again. So, he had hired an

ambulance, reasoning that you did not in New York have to be sick in order to take a ride in one.

Now, he was racing towards a first meeting with Ernest Hemingway, for which he had forsaken a whole afternoon's work.

It was time for the two men to meet.

Hemingway has long been regretting his agreement to rewrite *The Spanish Earth* for Ivens. After completing what he had considered to be his final draft, Ivens had returned it to him with notes, expecting something entirely new and reworked. That did not sit well, but Hemingway had done it because *la causa* was too important to throw away over such misunderstandings. So he had gone over it again and cut things and written others and moved it all around until he felt that Ivens would be sated.

The film was going well, too, even if he found it difficult to follow someone else's lead and then to write words to match what he saw on the screen. It was as if he were boxing and having to throw his combinations off the jab of his opponent.

Pauline knew how he felt, of course. He knew that she would. She knew because she had always been his best reader. And she knew about Gellhorn, too, and what it meant. She knew because she had been in Martha's position once, the woman pulling him away from his wife. And he knew that she knew that she was going to lose, and he knew that whatever was coming up between the pair of them was going to be nothing but painful.

He knew his sons missed him, and he missed them, too, even as he saw darker things roll in Greg. There were nights when Hemingway, as he fell asleep, thought and worried about 'Gig'. *He's a good shot and he'll be a fair man*, his narrator told him, *but he's just got to get that darkness down and under control.*

Patrick was fine, of course. He always would be. *He has that air about him*, his own narrator said. And Jack. Well, he regretted the whole thing of not being around Jack, 'Bumby' as they used to call him. The pain of going from Hadley, and of seeing his boy go with her, draped over him. *If things had been different*, the narrator tormented him, *and if you had been different – better – then you would all still be together, maybe, in Paris.*

He was back in the thrust of things. 'The eye of it!' he had shouted once as bullets flew around him in Aranjuez. He had stayed alive through that first war, and this new war in turn had kept him alive and reinvigorated him. Martha, when he rolled over one morning and pushed himself up against her, made the remark that there was some lead back in his pencil, and he had to laugh at that.

Now, there was the film. It was supposed to be Ivens's thing, but he felt as if it were one of his own children – or, at least, a nephew or a niece of some sort. He knew that his name would sell it, and sell *la causa*, and he knew that it was also going to be damn good, even if he could not figure out how it was all going to come together.

Martha loved it, of course, and he thought that he loved her. He hoped that she loved him, too. She had been speaking of the film with Eleanor Roosevelt and it had been arranged for them to take it to the White House in a few weeks, and all they had to do to finish it was to get the voice down for the narration.

It was Ivens who had chosen the kid, a recommendation from Blitzstein, and he was said to be some kind of *wunderkind* on the New York stage. Hemingway knew little about him and did not care to know much more. Who was he but another actor, some marionette who walked about in dress clothes and spoke the words of other men? It was a profession that he saw no honour in.

But Blitzstein had vouched for the kid, saying he was *The Shadow*,

and Greg and Patrick loved that show, so Hemingway had assented to what seemed like a good idea.

Welles walked into the screening room and looked around. He saw Ivens first but then caught a glimpse of Hemingway. The writer began to lumber over, and Welles walked forwards, his hand out-stretched. Hemingway held a glass of whiskey between clenched fingers.

'Hello,' Welles said, swallowing. He reached out and shook hands with Hemingway. *I'm shaking hands with him*, he thought. 'I'm Orson.'

'Papa.'

'It's a pleasure to meet you.' Welles looked at Hemingway and realised how drawn the writer looked, despite his skin being a deep brown from the suns of Spain and Florida. There was a deep exhaustion in his eyes and he was overweight, too, his shirt collar open and his tie loose. There was sweat on his brow, beaded onto the skin above his eyes, and his nose was red and raw. His voice was lighter and higher than he had imagined. The handshake, however, was strong.

'Likewise.'

'I'm a big fan of your books, particularly *Death in the Afternoon*.'

'Thank you.'

Hemingway turned and walked back over to Ivens, the brief conversation over. Welles looked around, then took off his jacket and placed it on the back of one of the chairs. 'Do you have a script I can see?' he called over to the two men.

Hemingway turned. There was a look of irritation on his face. *Who is this kid*, he thought, *to interrupt my conversation with my director?*

'One moment, Orson,' Ivens said, before he and Hemingway went back into a huddle.

'OK,' said Welles, causing the two men to turn once more, 'I'll just wait here until you're ready.'

The two men turned away from Welles again, and Welles sat in one of the chairs. He leaned his head back and turned it, closing his eyes a little so he could still watch the others. He saw the pair compare notes, and Hemingway put his finger on his page to show Ivens something, then pushed down in a similar spot on the page in Ivens's hand.

They were eventually ready to start, and Welles began to walk over to the recording booth.

'One moment,' said Ivens with a weary exasperation, 'Papa wants to say some words.'

Hemingway cleared his throat. He had always hated public speaking and made a point almost always to never read any of his work in public, but he felt drawn to words. 'This is an important work,' he intoned, 'that we are here to do today. Fascism is a plague on Spain, and it will be a plague on Europe before too long.'

Welles looked around. The rest of the room stared entirely at Hemingway.

Hemingway continued. 'No true writer can live with fascism because it is a lie told by bullies. Once it is gone, it will have no history other than the bloody history of murder it has brought with it. Many people worked long and hard on this film, and some of them fell along the way.' He thought of José Robles, and of Dos Passos, and he felt their hands on his shoulders.

*I am so very sorry*, he thought, sadly, *but some trees have to be cut so that the forest can grow.*

Hemingway cleared his throat. 'It is very dangerous to write the

truth in war,' he said, 'and the truth is also very dangerous to come by. But there is now, and there will be from now on for a long time, war for any writer to go to who wants to study it. It looks as though we are in for many years of undeclared wars.'

The room went silent. Ivens walked up and patted Hemingway on the shoulder. 'Thank you, Papa,' he said.

Someone gave Welles a script, and he sat in the seats to read it. A few pages in, he took out a pencil, wet its tip and began to mark the paper.

Hemingway noticed and walked over. 'What are you doing?'

Welles nodded. 'I'm just noting a few things.'

'On my script?'

Welles closed the script and looked at it. 'I'm sorry. I didn't realise that this was your copy.'

'It's not. It's my script.'

Welles nodded. He deflected. 'I have to say, *Papa*, that it's very well written.'

'Thank you,' Hemingway said, then moved off. He went to the table at the back of the room where he took a fresh glass and poured two inches of whiskey into it.

'Joris, my dear,' Welles said, calling over the director. 'I have a few ideas.'

Ivens sat down. 'OK,' he said.

'Some of the language here is stuff that I think we can cut.'

'Like what?'

'You have this line: "Here are the faces of men who are close to death." I assume when this happens that you will have those faces on the screen, yes?'

'That is the plan.'

'Right. Well, why then don't we cut the line? If we're seeing their

faces on the screen at the same moment, might it be more eloquent to just see them?'

Ivens looked at Welles, then he looked at Hemingway. 'We will consider it,' he said.

'OK.'

After some toing and froing over the loading of the film into the projector, Ivens pressed his small hand on Welles's shoulder and said it was time for him to go into the booth. Welles walked over, the script in hand, stood behind the microphone and said, 'I've been ready for a while. I'll go when you want me to.'

'OK.'

The lights were dimmed, and then there was a flickering and whispering as the film started up and was played upon the screen. Welles cleared his throat.

'Are you OK, Orson?' asked Ivens.

Hemingway looked up at Welles as if regarding him for the first time. His eyes were small and dark in the dim light. He sipped from his glass.

'I'm good, thank you,' said Welles.

The credits finished, and then there were voices singing in the film over the dry and hard Spanish landscape and then the men who worked it, whose faces were also dry and hard.

There was a horse walking across arid ground. A broken, desiccated tree on worthless, unirrigated ground. A long, long shot of livestock walking the edge of a dead field. People walking in the distance. More shots of the land. A smoking chimney.

'I really think we should cut some of this down,' said Welles. 'There's so much here that we don't need. I think we should go straight to the music and tell people of the beauty of Spain and its people.'

Hemingway waved Welles over to a small table, then took out a pencil. 'What parts', he said, 'do you think we don't need?'

Welles opened his script and put it on the table, spreading out its pages. 'Look,' he said, 'we can cut this part about the faces.'

'Why?'

'I don't think it's needed.'

'Why not?'

'Because we're going to be showing the faces on the screen at the same moment. It's enough to just have that.'

Hemingway looked at the script, then up at the image being projected on the screen. 'You know,' he said. 'You might be right. I guess I never thought about it that way.'

'It's good writing, but it's *part* of the whole thing, not the *whole* thing.'

'I get what you're saying.'

'OK.'

Welles moved back towards the booth. Hemingway yelled over to Ivens. 'The kid wants to take some bits out about the faces. Are you OK with that?'

Ivens yelled back. 'Are you?'

Hemingway glowered. 'Let's just get this done with.'

Welles stood in the booth. He put his hand to his ear, placed it on the headphones. He took a breath and began to speak again.

There was bread now and mentions of wine and onions. Welles felt his stomach shake in hunger. He saw the people on screen walk between Spanish villages, and he thought they should cut the parts about food in order to make front and centre the military value of the bridge between those villages.

The small, cramped room began to fill with furling cigarette smoke.

Welles looked down at the script. 'Hmm...' he said, noncommittally, as he looked at his lines.

Hemingway heard the noise. He glowered.

Welles began to read from the paper. He spoke the first few lines, then held up his hand. 'It's not working,' he said.

Ivens looked over. 'Not working?'

Welles shook his head. 'No, no. Not at all.'

Ivens looked at Hemingway, then looked back at Welles.

Welles missed the glance in Hemingway's direction.

Ivens walked halfway across the room to Welles, and he looked over to the young actor. 'What's not working?' he asked.

'There's too much narration here. Wouldn't it be better...' He walked over to Ivens and thrust the script under the small lamp between them, 'If we just cut *this* and *this*...' He turned over a couple of pages. 'And this.'

Hemingway glowered. He coughed and cleared his throat. 'Who the fuck is this?' he demanded, with a growl.

Welles turned in his direction. 'Who the fuck is who?' he asked.

'Who's this damn faggot who runs an art theatre, and who is he to tell me how to write narration!?'

Welles raised an eyebrow, then walked back to the microphone at the other side of the room. 'Very well,' he said.

Ivens started the picture again. He offered up a silent prayer.

Hemingway got to his feet, and he yelled, 'Who is this fucking asshole from the theatre who is over there trying to teach me about writing narration?'

Welles pulled the headphones from his ears and stepped outside the booth. 'I'm sorry?'

Hemingway began to walk towards him. 'I said,' he repeated, 'who are you to teach me about narration?'

'Well...' Welles let the word hover in the air deliberately. The very intonation of it began to incense Hemingway. *The education of this prick*, thought the writer, *and the gall!*

Hemingway got closer, moving to within six feet of Welles. He hissed, saying slowly, 'When you say the word "infantry", you sound like a cocksucker taking a breath.'

'Right.'

Hemingway stood in front of Welles, his fists by his side. His script was rolled and tightened in one of them like a police baton. The tang smell of whiskey lay on his breath. 'Say the damn words as we – *I* – wrote them, you prick.'

'Very well.' Welles turned and stepped back into the recording booth, then turned again to face Hemingway at a distance. Welles thought of the angry bulls in Spain, and he brought up his hands and flopped and flapped his wrists. He wanted now to anger the writer. 'Oh, Mr Hemingway,' he said, with a lisp, 'you're so brave and so strong, with all that hair on your chest! I just hope you go easy on me when the time comes!'

Hemingway's eyes widened, and he gasped and went for Welles. 'That's it, you big bastard!' he yelled. He threw a wide, loose hook that Welles, bringing up his hands, caught on his arms and shoulder, before the younger man barrelled forward, his head in the face of Hemingway, and grabbed the writer by his lapels.

Welles was taller and began to smother Hemingway with his weight. Hemingway grabbed Welles by the waist and tried to haul him around. He pushed him away and threw a hook to Welles's stomach, but then Welles grabbed him again and pushed him around and up against the chairs.

'It's my narration, you fucking prick,' said Hemingway, his voice muffled in Welles's chest.

Welles wrapped his arm around Hemingway's neck and tried to knee him in the groin. 'I'm. The. Fucking. Narrator,' he said, between swipes.

To the side of them, still on the screen, the Spanish Civil War continued to play on celluloid.

'Fuck you!' yelled the stronger Hemingway, pushing Welles back against the wall. 'I'm the writer here!'

A breathless Welles leaned forward onto Hemingway's back. 'I write!'

The lights went on.

'Will you two stop it?' said Ivens, stepping towards them. He placed a hand on each man's shoulder and lightly pushed at them. They relaxed.

Hemingway disengaged and took a step back. He wiped at his mouth. 'You write?'

Welles looked at him, his mouth open and gasping. His cheeks pulled in air, then pushed it out again like a pair of broken bellows. His hair tumbled down over his eyes. 'Yes.'

'Oh, I didn't know.' Hemingway's face shifted, and a smile came to its surface. 'I didn't know you write.'

Welles looked at him. 'Pretty much everything I act in, dear boy.'

'I never knew.'

'And I fought a bull once, too. In Seville.'

Hemingway pulled up a wooden chair and sat down. He reached over to the wooden table, took the bottle of whiskey and looked down at it.

Welles came and sat next to him. The collar of his shirt was loose and, at its other end, it hung like a fringe over the top of his trousers.

Hemingway looked him up and down. 'That was a good fight,' he said, smiling.

'You think so?'

Hemingway shrugged. 'Drink?' he asked. He took the bottle and, upending it, poured some of its contents into his mouth. He pushed the bottle into Welles's hands. 'Drink,' he repeated.

'Sure,' Welles said, taking the bottle and drinking. He took two massive swallows and then handed the bottle back.

'Any good at it?' asked Hemingway.

'At what? The writing or the bullfighting?'

'The bullfighting.'

Welles laughed. 'The worst they'd ever seen. They called me *El Americano*. If I had done it two years before, you'd have had to put me in your book as the most hopeless bullfighter ever seen on the soils of Spain.'

The two of them began to laugh. Hemingway brought down his meaty hand on Welles's shoulder. Welles threw a light, joking punch at the writer's midriff.

# ACT TWO

# A DANCE OF BULLS
# (1938 TO 1961)

# 7

# THE THEATRE OF THE AIR
# (1938 TO 1940)

It was a Sunday evening in Newark, New Jersey, and the Sneddon family had just finished dinner. It was October, and the air outside their apartment was cold. Thick condensation had formed on the windows. Their bellies were full and they were tired. Sleep was not far away.

'Open that,' someone from the family said, and then one of their members stood, went to the window and opened it. Cold air with the scents of fumes and smoke began to flow into the apartment.

'It's time for the show,' someone else said and then, like millions of other Americans, they gathered around the Bakelite radio, switched it on, saw its yellow light brighten and glow and heard the humming whine beginning over static as the aerial ebbed into life.

The father, Bill Sneddon, went into the kitchen and took two ice-cold beers from the icebox, popped off their caps and went back into the room with the radio. He handed one of the beers to his wife Mabel, then sat in the easy chair next to the table on which the radio stood.

Bill Jr, his son, sixteen years old and the same height as his father,

looked at the beer in Bill Sneddon's hand. There was a peach-fluff beard beneath the boy's mouth and his long nose heightened the sharpness of the face and the adolescent thinness of his shoulders.

'Can I have one?' the boy asked, expectantly.

The father shook his head. 'Only when you can buy your own.'

Someone began to turn the dial, scooting across the channels, looking for their regular show. There was the *skrrr* of static, then a grasp of garbled voices, as the signal moved across the frequencies.

*Skrrr*… voices… *Skrrrr*… voices… *Skrrr*… voices.

A few gasped syllables came from the speakers and the hand turning the dial stopped.

Something was wrong.

Something was terribly wrong.

'Good heavens,' said the voice, tight and strained, 'something's wriggling out of the shadow like a grey snake. Now it's another one, and another. They look like tentacles to me. There, I can see the thing's body. It's large, large as a bear and it glistens like wet leather. But that face, it… Ladies and gentlemen, it's indescribable. I can hardly force myself to keep looking at it. The eyes are black and gleam like a serpent. The mouth is V-shaped with saliva dripping from its rimless lips that seem to quiver and pulsate. The monster or whatever it is can hardly move. It seems weighed down by… possibly gravity or something. The thing's raising up. The crowd falls back now. They've seen plenty. This is the most extraordinary experience. I can't find words… I'll pull this microphone with me as I talk. I'll have to stop the description until I can take a new position. Hold on, will you please, I'll be right back in a minute.'

A piano started to play.

Bill stood up. He looked at Mabel. He looked at their two smallest kids. 'What was that?' he asked.

'I don't know, Bill,' Mabel replied. 'I really don't know.'

An announcer came back on. They said they were broadcasting live from Grovers Mill, New Jersey.

'What is that?' said Bill. 'Fifty miles from here?' He looked at his son, with his glasses, his head always buried deep in books. The boy was as ungainly as a stork, uneasily wearing a body not yet filled out for manual work. 'Do you know?'

'I guess.'

Bill looked at his family, then he leaned over to Mabel. 'Maybe put some things to one side, OK? Just in case. I want to listen to this.'

He reached over and turned the volume dial, heard the tinny speakers on the radio become almost overpowered with the now-garbled sound. 'Quiet, everyone,' he said.

The voice, again, began to describe the scene. There were police now, about thirty of them, and they were drawing up a cordon around a pit. The crowd was staying back.

There was a hissing sound.

The voice: 'A humped shape is rising out of the pit. I can make out a small beam of light against a mirror. What's that? There's a jet of flame springing from the mirror, and it leaps right at the advancing men. It strikes them head on! Good Lord, they're turning into flame!'

Screams. Shrieks. The eruption of fire.

An explosion.

'The woods... the barns... the gas tanks of automobiles... it's spreading everywhere. It's coming this way. About twenty yards to my right...'

Bill turned the radio down. He whispered to his wife. 'Pack those bags. Whatever's happening, they'll aim for New York next, and we'll be in the way.'

She heard the urgency in his voice. She took the two smallest with her into the bedroom and began packing.

Bill clicked his fingers at Bill Jr. 'You stay here while I get the car,' he said. 'Keep listening.'

'OK, Dad.'

Bill Sneddon eased the car out into the street. Mabel was in the back with the girls, Bill Jr was in the front with him, holding a map.

'Where are we going, Dad?'

'Out of town.' Bill did not know where. All he knew was that he wanted to be out of New Jersey, soon.

He noticed that there were so many vehicles on the street that he could barely move. People walking overtook them. He saw cases and bags piled high in the backs of cars and trucks, and he knew that they were also leaving as quickly as they could.

Some people sat outside their homes, on stairs and stoops, talking amongst themselves. They looked unconcerned. Some shrugged.

It had been going on for nearly forty minutes.

Sneddon yelled at them. 'The Martians!' he screamed into the cold night air. 'The Martians are coming!'

At around the same time, at a church in Harlem, about twenty miles from Newark, a similar kerfuffle exploded. Neither its congregants nor the Sneddons knew each other. These were lives that would never flow together.

The service was coming to a close when the doors flew open at the back and Mrs Jones, a local lady known and thought of well in the neighbourhood, came running in. She began to yell at everyone in the room, her thick, fleshy arms shaking in the air.

'New York is being destroyed!' she screamed, tears rolling down her voice. Her sobbing was relentless and thick. 'It's the end of the world! Go home and prepare to die!'

Mrs Jones had been listening to the radio, too.

Later that night, Orson Welles went into the back area of the theatre, which he and Houseman had set up months before, and tried to convince people that the country had been panicked by *The War of the Worlds*.

No one believed him. They did not think that the police had entered the booth during the broadcast and threatened to arrest him or that anyone could have taken the show, with its multiple warnings, as anything other than a radio play. They did not believe that thousands across America had fled their homes in fear of an alien invasion.

Glumly, Welles took Joseph Cotten by the arm and led him outside, then down to Times Square. He pointed at the ticker running across one of the buildings, the one that gave New Yorkers the news. It read: ORSON WELLES TERRIFIES THE WORLD.

'See,' he said, sadly, with fear in his voice. 'Do you see what we did, Joe?'

Welles went back to CBS the next day and sat in an office with the producers and with Houseman as they worked to write up a press release. The phone rang continuously, and each time, they answered it, reassured the caller that they would be putting out a statement later that day and then went back to sitting around and waiting for something to happen.

One of the directors of the station came in. It was someone whom

Welles had never seen before, and he thought he looked as anonymous as the rest, so unknowable that the young actor and director wondered if this director even had a name.

The director put his hands on the large conference table and leaned forward, fixing Welles and Houseman with a direct, eye-grabbing glare. 'Why did you do it, Orson?' he asked. 'Why did you do it *that* way?'

Welles shrugged. 'I don't know what answer to give you.'

'Well, why did you write it as if it was real in the first place?'

Houseman leaned over. 'Actually, it was Howard—'

Welles tapped Houseman on the arm. 'It's OK, House,' he said. He turned to the director. 'I wrote it, because I wanted to scare people. I obviously did not intend to scare them *that* well.'

The phone rang. No one answered it. They let it ring out.

'Now,' the director said, 'we're doing the best that we can. We're putting out reminders every forty minutes that last night was just a show. There's not much else we can do. I think you will have to try to act contrite.'

Welles looked down. He looked like a small boy caught stealing. 'I guess we can try that,' he said. 'House?'

Houseman looked over. 'I think we *should* try it, Orson,' he said. 'OK.'

The phone rang again. They ignored it.

The director looked at Welles and Houseman. 'There are newspaper men outside, and we've already fired someone in the mailroom who thought it would be a good idea to bring up some Mars bars as a special delivery.' The director took off his glasses and pinched his nose. 'You two scared half of America last night. And the other half wants something done to the pair of you.'

The phone rang again. They ignored it.

'So what we do now', said the director, 'is wait. The lawyers are expecting to be busy with all the lawsuits that will come in.'

'Lawsuits for what?' asked Houseman, with genuine curiosity.

'You scared half of the country. Someone, somewhere, is going to sue over that.'

'Oh.'

The director shook his head. 'They're saying people died, Orson. Suicides. Car accidents. God knows, but I bet a poor, fed-up wife somewhere figured she could get away with shooting her husband if the world was coming to an end. Do you know how serious this is?'

'I didn't know.' Welles looked down at his lap. 'I didn't know,' he said, again.

The phone rang again. They ignored it.

The director looked at them. 'That's it for the show,' he said. 'We're pulling the Mercury Theatre's contract for the shows. We're going to hold off on what we haven't yet broadcast until all this has blown over, and then maybe do them.'

The phone rang again. The director snatched it up. 'What!?' he asked, with exasperation, into the handset. 'What!?' He waited. His face sank. He put his fingers to his forehead. He nodded, grimly, and put his hand on the table in front of him. 'Oh, Jesus,' he said, then put the phone down.

He looked at Welles and Houseman. 'And now there's a bomb threat,' he said, with a great and exasperated sigh. 'We need to get out of here.'

Welles and Houseman were in the ladies' bathroom, sat on wooden chairs that they had carried in with them after the bomb threat.

They had been in the bathroom for about forty minutes, both profoundly irritated with the sound of water dripping into one of the
sinks, that continual tapping of drops against porcelain.

Both were scared. They thought about the lawsuits and the legal
fees and were not sure how much they would be protected by CBS.
There had been also the threat of legal, criminal charges, although
no one could be quite sure what they would be charged with or how
successful such endeavours might be.

'I doubt anyone died, Orson,' Houseman said, eventually, his
accent having regained its usual clipped cadence. Thinking clearly
in emergencies was a Houseman specialty. 'I think it's all bunkum.'

Welles stood up. The wooden chair had caused his back to creak
and ache. He walked around the bathroom for a few moments, then
stopped and splashed some water on his face.

'Yes, I suppose so,' he said, with some disappointment. 'But imagine if we really have! That really would be some kind of magic
trick, wouldn't it?'

'I suppose it would.'

'How long do you think they'll keep us in here?'

'I have no idea.'

'Well, we have to get to the Mercury to rehearse.'

'We're not rehearing today, Orson. Maybe any other day. No one
will touch us.'

Welles looked over at Houseman. 'You're wrong, House.'

'I'm wrong?'

'Very much so. We just became the hottest names in America.'
Welles reached into his overcoat, which was slung over the back
of his wooden chair, and took out a cigar and a match. He lit the
former with the latter and sucked down a lungful of smoke. 'Good

news or bad news, this is all good publicity. We'll sell tickets, even if we cannot sell the show any more.'

'Let's see, Orson.'

'Mark my words, House. Mark my words.' The smoke from the cigar began to fill the tiled room.

'I don't think you're allowed to do that in here,' said Houseman.

'Nonsense. It covers up all the smells.' Welles puffed on the cigar.

'What does Virginia think?'

'Ginny?' said Welles. 'She's fine. She's upstate, preparing for the baby. She thinks it's all kind of hilarious, and she cannot wait to see what comes next.'

'You married a good woman.'

Welles looked at Houseman, raised an eyebrow. 'I rather think', he said, 'that she would agree with you on that.'

There was a knock at the door. It opened a little, then the director put his head through the small gap. 'I have news,' he said. 'The Mercury Theatre is off the air.'

Houseman and Welles deflated with the sad news.

The director cracked a smile. 'However, the soup company Campbell's has come onboard. They're going to sponsor the whole thing. They think you two are a good investment.'

Welles and Houseman spoke in unison. 'Really?'

'Really. You'll have to change the name, of course. It's *The Campbell Playhouse* from now on, and there's going to be some things that you still need to work out. But the upshot of it all is that you're going to have some bigger budgets and better stars, even as you have to sell soup in order to do it. I'll leave you to discuss things.'

After the director had gone, Welles and Houseman stood, leaned on their chairs and looked at each other.

'What do you think?' said Welles, his cigar now burned halfway down.

'I think', said Houseman, a smile playing on his face, 'that if we can sell the end of the world, then we should have no problem in selling soup!'

The remit of the reformulated *Mercury Theatre on the Air* was to produce, under its new name, fresh and modern adaptations of classic literature, beginning with *Rebecca*. The shows were an hour long, produced once a week and transmitted live over the air on Friday evenings.

For Welles, the new workload added to his exhaustion. In addition to the shows on the radio, he and Houseman continued to run the Mercury Theatre in New York, with Welles providing its artistic direction and Houseman begrudgingly saddled with its increasingly chaotic financial state. In addition, Welles continued as the voice of *The Shadow*.

At home, Welles's family life was beginning to crumble. He began affairs with ballet dancers and actresses, and, despite the birth of his daughter Christopher, he continued to work long and Benzedrine-fuelled hours, writing and rehearsing the theatre shows during the day and supervising their technical brilliance at nights. He slept often in the stalls of the theatre, kept using the ambulance to hare around the Manhattan streets and developed a prodigious appetite for alcohol and food.

In November 1938, the Mercury Theatre unveiled his production of *Danton's Death*, which closed after just twenty-one performances, leaving the company heavily in debt. The company began to scrabble for money.

The radio shows continued but shifted in production gradually

across the country, as Welles and his theatre troupe toured the cities: Boston, Philadelphia, Chicago.

Eventually, Hollywood called. Welles ignored the call as long as he could. He said one day, out of the side of his mouth to Houseman, 'When you honestly don't want to go, the deals get better and better.'

He gave in. He went over and began developing projects. He kept working on the radio.

They adapted more. Critical acclaim. The show heard everywhere.

More productions. *Mutiny on the Bounty, Beau Geste, Les Misérables.*

And then, in December 1939, the most modern adaptation of all those put on by Welles and *The Campbell Playhouse*: *A Farewell to Arms.*

The end of December 1939 saw Houseman arrive in Los Angeles, go to the Chateau Marmont to see Welles, not find him there, and head instead to the studio.

The city was never cold, and the Romanian-born Englishman, now thirty-seven years old, felt warm in his cloying suit as his taxi took him down Sunset Boulevard. His overcoat lay on the seat beside him and his cases were in the back. Houseman loosened his tie, closed his eyes, laid his head on the top of the seat and began to doze. His nose felt stuffed, and he could feel the faint signals of an incoming migraine. His shoulders slumped involuntarily. Dark, deep hands began to pull him down into sleep.

The Mercury Theatre was waning. *Danton's Death* had been disastrous, with nothing ever really working – neither the cast, nor the script, nor the elaborate technology that underpinned the entire production. Now, there seemed little hope of getting Welles back

to New York in order to right the ship, which was why, clutching a new deal that might save everything, Houseman had made the trip to California.

It was late when he got to the studio. After the driver had shaken him by the shoulder, then deposited him and his bags outside, Houseman went into the building, left what he could at reception and went up to watch through the glass the recording of *A Farewell to Arms*.

Houseman had, evidently, come at the end of the broadcast, and he saw Welles and Katharine Hepburn as they finished off the story of Frederic Henry and Catherine Barkley. He wondered what Hemingway would have made of it all.

The thought slipped from his mind when he looked more closely at Welles, of whom he had not set eyes upon in weeks. He thought Welles looked worse than usual, so unkempt that it was as if everything that had once been controlled in him had somehow blown out as if a gasket had burst. The never-taut face had become puffy and slack, and his stomach had started to brim over the waistband of his trousers. His hair was longer and unkempt, and he wore a beard, and despite the low intensity of the ending of *A Farewell to Arms*, his brow was shiny with sweat. Houseman suspected the Benzedrine.

A light flickered in the control booth, and it indicated that there were less than five minutes to go before the play came off the air. Houseman saw the listing of Welles's body now, as if it had been held totally upright for far too long and was now beginning to fall in on itself in sections. Welles put his hand on the microphone stand, holding on to it as if it were some kind of staff, and he put his hand on Hepburn's shoulder.

Houseman listened in.

'It has been a remarkable evening,' Welles told Hepburn. 'Before it, I had never had the pleasure of your acquaintance. And it is a tragedy to me that in four minutes or so, you will be gone out of my life!'

Hepburn smiled. It was a Hollywood smile, vacant and carrying the charm of a pleasing billboard. She spoke, and her voice carried that familiar low burr. 'Why, thank you, Orson,' she said. 'It's been just splendid to be here with you on *The Campbell Playhouse*, acting out the part of Catherine Barkley in Ernest Hemingway's *A Farewell to Arms*!'

Welles tapped Hepburn on the shoulder and then he turned his body fully into the microphone and began the sign-off, asking the audience to take care of themselves over the weekend. Maybe, he suggested, they should try a nice can of Campbell's soup?

Afterwards, once Hepburn had got into a car and gone, Welles and Houseman sat in a small office at the back of the studio. Welles had removed his tie and sat, sipping warm pineapple juice. He looked spent, as if his body were too big for everything inside of it, and he was wearing it like a baggy, over-large suit.

'It was very generous of you to do that after Hemingway replaced you on the Spanish film.'

Welles shrugged. 'Did you hear it?' he asked.

'A bit,' said Houseman. 'In the car on the way over. And then I caught the end in the studio. It went well.'

'It went OK,' Welles said. 'But Hepburn... She's a talented amateur, but she'll never be a professional in a hundred years. Embarrassing.'

Houseman flinched, but he was used to the occasional, uncharitable barb. He wondered what the boy genius, now a husband and father, said about him when he was not around. He could guess, of

course, but even then he would not want to know the result of his thoughts. 'Did you see Ginny and Christopher?' he asked, changing the subject.

'I did. They're in Chicago right now, with her parents. And I'm back here, trying to keep it all together.'

Houseman flinched again. 'We need to talk about that, Orson.'

'Oh, House.' Welles leaned back and stretched out. He let out a small groan like a ship brushing the wall of a port. 'There's always something to speak about, some publicist or agent or actor or playwright or composer or set-builder that wants something from us.'

'That's true.'

'Can you handle it? I do the art, remember, and you do what you can to make the business run on time. Or as close to on time as you can.'

Houseman flinched a third time. 'I like to think I'm more than that, Orson,' he said. 'I *am* more than that. It's me who gets these plays working, too, and I bring in the guest stars, get them ready, get their contracts negotiated.'

Welles sat up. He pointed a finger at Houseman, and he smiled. 'That's because you started us with that ridiculous "guest star clause" that means we need a different movie star each week. It's no longer the Mercury.'

'Of course it is. It's the new flavour of the Mercury.'

'Which is what? Chicken soup? Cream of tomato? Asparagus?' Welles raised an eyebrow, fixed Houseman with a quizzical stare.

'People still call it *The Orson Welles Show*.'

'Well, that's good.' Welles patted himself, then looked in his shirt pocket. He took out a box of matches, then pulled from somewhere a cigar. 'See that, House?' he asked. 'That is magic.'

Houseman felt the gulf between him and Welles. 'That's all you

ever wanted it to be, Orson,' he said. '*The Orson Welles Show*, and we are all bit players and supports to your genius.'

'You sound like everyone else, House, although I like the idea of being a "boy genius". You should tell more jokes like that.'

'If I sound like everyone else, and everyone else is saying the same thing, Orson, then maybe the problem is with you and not with everyone else.'

Welles lit the cigar. 'I never said there was a problem.'

'I'm not your support, Orson. I'm your partner.'

Welles drew on the cigar. He and Houseman could hear the crinkle of its fire. He took it out and licked his lips. 'It's 30 December, John, and tomorrow will be the last day of the 1930s. War is going on in Europe and, I dare say, it will impact on us soon. And you are here.'

'I am.'

'Because you have something?'

'I don't know if you want it.'

Welles shifted in his chair. 'What is it?'

'A new theatre arrangement. The Theatre Guild wants to buy into the Mercury. They're calling it a partnership, but this will open us up. New subscription lists, new theatres, more resources.'

'I have a deal with RKO. They want me for something, for anything. It's getting quite tiresome, but all they do is keep offering me more money.'

'This deal is done. I just need your assent and signature.' Houseman sat down.

'Do you have the papers?'

'They're downstairs.'

'I can't sign anything if they're downstairs.'

'I came to see you.'

Welles snorted. 'Did you?'

'Yes.' Houseman took out a cigarette and lit it. 'Those things', he said, pointing to Welles's cigar, 'are for little boys attempting to be men.' He held up his cigarette. '*These* are for the grown-ups.'

Houseman tapped the table. 'It's a good deal,' he said. 'We're putting in $10,000, half of it in services, but the budget will be four times that. And we get to tour their theatres.'

'But they'll only sign if it's me.'

Houseman sighed. 'That's correct.'

'Well, I guess I am a boy genius, then. What do they want?'

'Shakespeare. Lots of him.'

'I'll think about it.'

'I already know your answer.'

'I'm sure you do.'


Welles called Houseman the next day at his room in the Chateau Marmont. It was 10.30 a.m., and Houseman was packing his bags for the trip back to New York. He worked out that if he could leave in the afternoon, he might get to Idlewild for the evening, which would leave him enough time to get somewhere in Harlem where he could drink and smoke as one decade rolled into another.

Welles did not bother saying hello, but Houseman knew the voice. It was less bombastic than when it was onstage, but there was no error in his identification of it. Welles said simply, 'No. No to all of it. No to the deal.'

'You're staying here?'

'They're offering me everything,' Welles explained. 'And I explained your deal to them this morning, and they offered me a lot more.'

'You leveraged our theatre against a movie deal for yourself?'

'I did it, because the Mercury is done, House. We did everything that we wanted to do with it. And we achieved everything we thought we would, and everything we aimed for.'

'They offered you more?'

Welles's voice became animated. It was as if he were trying to make Houseman see something obvious and readily apparent. 'They offered me *everything*,' he said. 'The whole railroad set. Writer, director, actor. Choice of material, too. I'm looking at a number of projects. Maybe I'll even do that *Heart of Darkness* we always talked about. Or the *Ambersons*.'

Houseman heard the crackle on the line. He knew Welles was only a few hundred yards away, probably in a villa just beyond the pool. There was probably also a showgirl or ballerina sleeping in the single bedroom in that villa, the scent of her perfume still hanging in the air.

'Do you have anything to say, House?'

Houseman could hear the crackle of Welles's breath on the line and the voice with its strangely consistent tone like that of an air siren in the fog. 'I'm going back to New York tonight, Orson,' he said, eventually. 'I can see now that there's nothing here for me.'

Welles's voice was flat. 'That might be a good idea, House,' he said. 'That might be a good idea.'

Houseman slowly, gently, put down the phone. He heard the soft click of the line disconnecting between the two of them.

The pair of them did not speak for some weeks. Welles stayed in California, where he worked on camera tests for *Heart of Darkness*. Houseman went back to New York, where he caroused as best as he could for a fortnight.

One day, Houseman was in the backroom of the Mercury Theatre.

He had realised that he would have to sell on the lease, he was look-ing at everything that now needed a new home, and he wondered where the time had gone. All those productions, all those nights on the stage. The Federal Theatre Project before all of that.

He opened the drawer of his desk and took out a bottle of brandy. It had been opened some time ago, and most of it was gone. House-man took a coffee cup and poured into it half an inch.

The door opened. Welles was standing there. He still looked puffy, but the beard and the hair were neater, and there was contrition in his eyes. He pointed at the bottle.

'Can I get one?'

'Sure, Orson.' Houseman found a second cup and filled it with an inch.

Welles took the drink, then sat down. He leaned across the wooden desk and tapped the cup against Houseman's, then raised it to his mouth. 'Happy New Year, I guess,' he said, one eye on his former partner.

'What do you want, Orson?'

'You know that I'm no good without you,' he said.

'I always knew that. Have you come to apologise?'

Welles grimaced. 'That's a hard thing to do. But I did come here to ask you something.'

Houseman looked around the office. 'It's always in this room that you come to ask me something. Maybe one day you'll just come here and tell me something instead. Or maybe you'll just apologise.'

Welles drank some of the brandy. He took out a cigar, lit it quick-ly and let the smoke furl into the air. 'Just like old times. Us here, drinking, a cigar. Me asking for something.'

'Sounds right.'

'It's an offer, House. No more theatre as our main thing, no big tours. The big time now.'

'Are you offering me Hollywood?'

Welles nodded. 'If you want it.'

'And *Heart of Darkness*?'

'Dead. They never really wanted it. They want me to make monster movies and frighten people. They want *The War of the Worlds*, live on the screen. I don't want that.'

'Is it time for a speech, Orson?'

'It is.' Welles stood and went to the window, the same one he had stood at countless times before. He looked down on the cold New York streets and at the people who shuffled along them in the snow, collars turned up, their faces hidden. He saw the steam from their breaths gasp out in little puffs and he saw the sliding steps of their feet on the icy tarmac.

Welles tapped the window. 'Have I ever told you', he said, 'that I once met Hitler?'

'You have.'

'I forget my audiences.' Welles turned back to the window. 'We were hiking as schoolboys through Austria with some budding Nazi teacher, and we came to a rally near Innsbruck. And I had the fortune – or the misfortune – to be sat for dinner that night alongside Adolf Hitler, who was really nothing more than the leader of a comical minority of nuts that no one took seriously. I remember his moustache, but that's all. He was more or less invisible to me.'

Welles laughed at some absurd thought. 'And now there's a war coming. It'll go through Europe first but have no doubt that we'll be drawn at some point into it. It's inevitable. And it's not about ideology but about power. So I want to make a thing about power,

House, and of how it can corrupt. And I want you to be there, along the way, to help me.'

Houseman stood, and he took the hand of Welles. The pair of them embraced, and it felt for that moment that they were still in the old times. It was like a romantic comedy, although never as easy, and reconciliations are invariably temporary. But it was good enough, at that moment, for the pair of them.

# 8

# WARS (1939 TO 1946)

Ernest Hemingway still woke each morning when it was early. It was, he said, because of the thin eyelids that made it impossible for him to sleep once they began to let through the light. And it did not matter then, nor did he care, about where he was or whose bed he was in, because if the air was still cool, he would go to his desk to sit and try to write 500 words.

Fitzgerald had once joked that he needed a new wife for each book, and that observation was appearing to hold true. Hemingway was doing everything in two lives. He was living with both Marty and with Pauline, shuttling between the two. He had Pauline at home in Key West, and Marty was everywhere else.

He knew what was happening in this rhyming of history, doing between Pauline and Marty what he had once done between Hadley and Pauline.

Back and forth.

Pauline, then Marty.

Marty, then Pauline.

Two lives, one family, one love.

He rotated between his family and the woman he loved. He wondered why they could not be one and the same.

When he was in Havana, he would stop at 1 or 2 p.m., and then he would go drink with Marty. He drank fifteen or sixteen scotch-and-sodas a day.

When he was in Key West, he would also stop at 1 or 2 p.m., and then he would play with his boys. He and Pauline just looked away from each other, the marriage dead but neither one yet able to call it over.

Pauline knew about Marty. She knew her husband's affections. She tried to save her marriage. She took them all away on trips – her, him, the boys. They did all the things that he loved. She wanted him to think about the old days. She wanted him to save them. She wanted their lives to fit back into what they had once been. But she failed, and she kept on failing. Eventually, she wrote to him and told him to be happy wherever he was if he could not be happy at home.

He went back to Spain three more times. He saw the war, the Republic beginning to crumble. All that should have been won was lost.

The Republicans were defeated in 1939, and he sat and wept as his friends and compatriots went into exile in France. And it was Marty who saw him weeping, and she fell in love with him because of it.

He thought about a new novel, this one about Spain and the people fighting for it. He wanted it to be about Spain. He wanted to write it in Spain, but Spain was now gone. He needed somewhere else. He looked over the water from Key West, and he saw Havana thirty miles away. It was the closest thing he saw to Spain. He decided that if he could not have the latter, then he would have the former.

He invited Gellhorn to live with him at his hotel, the Ambos

Mundos, and she saw him write. She saw that he lived nearly in squalor and in disarray, but she marvelled at him working. She looked for somewhere for them to live, found the Finca Vigía twelve miles from the centre of the city. It was $100 a month that he did not want to pay. She went ahead and did it.

The house was empty and broken in places. Flowers and plants ran through it. It was haunted by ghosts – a family that had lost all of its sons. Gellhorn wondered if it was the same with Hemingway. She cleaned it out. She brought in the mahogany furniture. She cleared the pool. She trimmed the gardens. She kept the large ceiba tree that she loved at the front.

She took Hemingway out there with her one day. She saw his shoulders relax. 'If we are not to have Spain,' he told her, 'then we can have each other here.'

'We will do great things,' Marty told him.

War broke out in Europe, and he told Pauline that it was over. A second wife and family now left behind. The second time he had sawn through that tendon.

He lived with Marty in Cuba, and he wrote. He called the book *For Whom the Bell Tolls*. He went to New York in March 1940 to see his play *The Fifth Column* on Broadway. He had written it in Spain, beneath the bombs and the bullets in 1938, but it was rewritten before production by a writer he hated. He hated the new version. He ignored it. It ran for eighty-seven performances, then closed.

Hemingway and Marty spun. Forged in war, they tried to find a new life in peace. Both of them figured it would be easy. Both of them were wrong. They drank, they fucked. She may or may not have had an abortion. It was an answer that she would never tell him. He could not understand. He felt that he knew little about her; she found no succour in him.

They worried about their health. They wrote to others about the weight they had lost. He went down to lower than 200 pounds. He boxed as much as he could, pushed his 41-year-old body as far as it would let him.

His boys came to Cuba to be with him. They all fell in love with Marty. Sixteen-year-old Bumby fell in love with her. Eleven-year-old Patrick fell in love with her. Nine-year-old Greg, with the nickname 'Gig', and those churning emotions, fell for her.

*For Whom the Bells Tolls* was released. It sold out everywhere. Seventy-five thousand copies, the public like locusts. The most famous writer in America hit his career peak. He bought the Finca Vigía.

It was November 1940 when the divorce came through from Pauline. He was free again, single. He and Marty waited seventeen days, then married in Wyoming when there was snow and ice on the ground. Air so cold that it hurt to breathe.

'We will do great things,' Marty told him.

They spent months in China, seeing the war from the east. They travelled all over, then came back to Cuba. He agreed to gather intelligence for the Americans. He agreed to gather intelligence for the Russians.

The alliances were different. The alliances were shifting. Those old friends were, as Dos Passos once relayed to him, murderers in different clothes.

Gellhorn went to Finland, to see that small country try to fight off the Russians. She loved the Finns and their willingness to live and die for their home. It reminded her of Spain. They reminded her of Spaniards.

The temperature made her despair. She hated the cold and the dark. Hers was a skin that craved to drink in sunlight. She thought about Hemingway and of Cuba. She thought of contentment.

Hemingway missed her like a hungry dog. He drank too much, and his mind wandered into dark places. He contemplated suicide. He put his wife to one side and replaced her with friends.

He got a boat and called it *Pilar*. It was the name of the daughter he never had. He and his hooligan friends fished and drank together on its decks. They took it out and floated it on the clear waters outside Cuba.

He agreed with the US government to patrol the waters off Cuba, looking for German submarines. He thought they would machine-gun any that came into the area. It was a suicidal plan that never came to pass. Mostly, they drank and sailed around. They killed nothing but fish. Everyone saw it for what it was, but only Marty had the courage to say it.

The US went into the war, and Hemingway did not go. His writing failed him. He failed at his writing. He struggled to put words down on the paper. Marty began to resent him for his absence from this larger *la causa*.

Marty was gone all the time. She went all over Europe, wrote for *Collier's*. She wrote more books – *Liana*, *The Heart of Another*. They were above love and sex and war. *Liana* was about a love triangle, and it poured salt into the wound of his guilt.

He began to doubt Marty. *Enemies stab you in the back*, he thought, *but it's friends that stab you in the heart.*

Marty had a short story called 'A Portrait of a Lady'. It was about a female journalist who used sex to get a story. His doubts about her deepened.

The drinking got harder, and the fun evaporated from it. He drank until he slept. He feared an empty bed.

He saw the darkness in Greg. He saw the boy one day try on Marty's clothes. He screamed at his son.

He sat with the boy. He knew the dark threads in the family. He tried to be calm. He tried to be understanding. 'We are a strange tribe, Gig,' he said, ruefully.

Marty came home. Her success reminded him of his failings. They fought. They made up. He still woke in the night to look at her in the cool Cuban air. He saw her on her back beneath the thin sheet, and he had the thought sometimes that she was dead, so he would place his hand on her leg, just below the knee, and then push it up to her thigh until it tickled her. And then she would roll over and away from him, and he was reassured that he and she were still alive.

They fought with words, and he cut her down to tears, and she wept, and he would rage at her until his anger was temporarily spent, and then they would make up.

One night, late in 1943, he was driving home with her from the centre of Havana when they started again, and they were screaming at each other over his drinking. He stopped the car, and she got out and sat in his seat and took the wheel to drive. The fight could have been over anything, but this time Hemingway reached over and he slapped her hard across the face.

Marty wiped the tears from her eyes, and she looked back at the road. Then she turned and glared at him and she held his eyes, and she spun the wheel and let the car slip off the road and into a tree.

Marty went away again. Another assignment, another trip. She wanted space between them. She felt there was more peace in war.

Hemingway wrote to her. He begged her to come back. The black dog came back for him. He felt it was all hopeless.

The narrator was still in his head. *Another one, old stick*, it told him. *Another one*. It explained nothing else. It did not need to.

She came home. She went back. She wanted to go to Europe. She wanted to go with *Collier's*.

He usurped her. He spoke to the editors. He was the bigger name. He volunteered to go.

*Collier's* hired him. *Collier's* put her to one side.

She knew it. She resented him for it. She knew the marriage was over.

He took a plane. He told her it was for men only. He lied. She knew he lied. She took a boat.

She knew he was bad for her. She figured that she was wrong for him.

He got to London in 1944. He felt this was his last war. He had survived Italy in 1918. He had survived Spain in 1937. *The third time's the charm*, he thought, ruefully. He prepared himself to be killed.

He got to London and stayed at the Dorchester.

He saw HER – Wife #4.

This was Mary. He would call her 'Miss Mary'. She was married to someone else. She was a war reporter for *TIME*. She had for him the right amount of bravery and the correct measure of deference.

He fell hard for her. He asked her to marry him. She knew he was already married. *He* knew that *she* was already married. He got drunk one night and placed a photograph of her husband in the toilet, then fired a pistol into it. Shards of porcelain everywhere, the rooms below flooded. She gasped. Her heart began to crack open to him.

It was May 1944, and the war was in the closing stages. There were still blackouts. He got into a car one night with Robert Capa, and they began to drive in the dark. He had no lights. He hit a metal water tanker. He smashed his head against the window. He got fifty-seven stitches there. He smashed his knees.

There was bleeding in his brain. His skull was fractured. His vision shimmered. His head ached. He lay in a hospital bed, blood

clotted into his thick beard. He could not bear the light. Another head injury following the ones in Italy, in Paris, on the boat off the Cuban coast.

Marty came to see him. She saw him in the bed, his head wrapped so thick in bandages that it looked like he was wearing a turban. She saw the nurses and their fussing over him. She laughed. She saw his rage. She saw the anger in his eye for a second before it slipped beneath the blurred focus. She caught herself.

She had heard about Mary Welsh. She looked at her husband in the bed, and she knew it was over. She saw him shake his fist at her.

'They will read my stuff long after the worms have devoured you,' he said.

She rolled her eyes. 'This is no way to behave when the world is at war,' she said. 'I'm leaving you.'

'Gellhorn,' he answered. She was no longer 'Marty'.

It was four days later, at the beginning of June, and he stood on a boat far back from the action. It was D-Day, and he saw from a distance the young boys and men running and scattering up the beaches at Normandy. He watched a thousand of them go at the Germans. He saw men drown under the weight of their packs, observed some of them cut down by gunfire. He saw all of it from a distance.

The brass would not let him go on the beaches. He was not sure if he wanted to go. He deferred to them.

The floor rocked beneath his feet. Far-off explosions and the *crack-crack-crack* of guns. He was removed for the first time in his life.

His head ached. He had to think hard for words. The stitches in his forehead itched and pulled. His ears rang without the sounds of bombs and bullets. He put his hand on his forehead and felt

the thick crescent-shaped scar from Paris, like a slug, on his skin, twenty years old now.

He closed his eyes of thought of Italy, of the explosion that rocked his head when he was a young man. He thought of running through the Italian trenches, carrying the wounded. He thought of the shell. He flexed the injured knee. He remembered the long scar on his foot.

The boat moved beneath his feet, rocked by the water, and he thought of Cuba. The fall on the boat, his head hitting the wooden floor. The anger, the confusion, the headaches that never really went away.

He was old now, and he felt it.

He saw the spray of the water as machine guns rattled the blue sea with bullets. He could smell the salt of the water.

He wondered about Gellhorn. He knew she was out there, closer to the action than he was. He looked at the ships on the sea, the ones in front of him, and he knew in his chest that she was somewhere amongst them.

His behaviour became erratic. He decided that he hated Gellhorn. He decided that he loved 'Miss Mary'. He decided that death was coming for him. All these thoughts running at him in his mind, like ghosts in stone corridors that leave you cold with their touch.

He felt that there was nothing else. He felt that it was all hopeless. He felt the urge to expire, high above the skies of Europe, in a bomber plane over Germany. He sat in the cold, and he breathed air tainted with the smell of diesel, and he saw the lights of the towns and cities below. He welcomed death. He welcomed the chance to go out at his full strength before age would weaken and disable him.

He wanted to go.

He went back into France with Patton's Third Army. He managed to find a German motorcycle with its sidecar. He tore with it through the roads of rural France. Some retreating Germans fired upon him, and he swerved into a ditch where he fell and hit his head on a rock.

He crawled away from the motorcycle and lay in the long grass. He watched the sun travel across the sky, its light shifting through the branches and the leaves. He thought of a Japanese word he knew: *komorebi*. The act of sunlight passing through trees.

There was a metal canteen that he drank from throughout the day. He slipped into unconsciousness here and there. He fought to stay awake. The light made his head ache. Sounds stretched and became warped. He thought of God, and he hated her, too.

He feared being found by Germans, but no one came; they had all retreated. He lay in the heat and the sun until it started to go cold.

He got up, eventually, when it was dark, and he stumbled back to the road. He started up the motorcycle again. He tore back through the roads, dried blood in his hair and on his skin. He felt the warm air flow over his hands. He laughed. The pain sat at the back of his head.

He met some French Resistance somewhere, and he persuaded them to put him in charge. He led them into Mont-Saint-Michel, where the people thought he was an American general. He carried a gun, and they showed him where three German soldiers were hiding in a crypt. He got some grenades, pulled out their pins and threw them into the building. He killed the soldiers in the crypt. The villagers rewarded him and his men with champagne. They went somewhere to eat, where a bomb erupted, and he sat and continued to feast while all those around him ran and hid.

He and his men cleared the roads of mines. They sought to make

it safe for the soldiers. He abandoned his war reporter clothing for a military uniform.

He went to a hotel a few nights later in Rambouillet where he got into an argument over rooms with a war reporter from the *Chicago Sun-Times* named Bruce Grant. A young newsman called Andy Rooney looked at him with disdain. Hemingway turned and invited Grant out into the gardens to fight. Grant refused to come out. Hemingway went back into the ballroom and slugged him. Soldiers pulled them apart.

He got to Paris and liberated his favourite bookshop, then he went to the Ritz and liberated its wine cellar. He met a young soldier in his hotel named J. D. Salinger and gave him some advice on writing. He saw Miss Mary, and he told her that he wanted to start a new family with her. He hoped that they might have a daughter together. She saw that he drank too much. She uncovered her heart a little more. She saw something vast and elemental in his being. She saw the troubled waters that ran through him.

He told tall tales. He began to believe his own legend. He talked of his own bravery. He talked of all the men he had killed in all the wars he had been in, even if they were all ghosts. He spoke about how he hated fascists. He thought of all they had taken from him. He thought of Robles in Spain, and he thought of Dos Passos.

*You are very sorry*, the narrator told him.

He heard that Bumby was a prisoner: shot down, injured, held in Germany. He developed a plan to go and get him back. Nobody else wanted to be part of his suicide mission.

He rampaged across France and into Belgium. It was now late 1944, and he was at Hürtgen Forest just over the border into Germany.

It was the closest thing to hell. Trees burning, darkness. Dead

bodies all around. Everyone running in one direction, then another. No clear orders. He felt it was time to die there. Eighteen days of time distilled into madness.

He took a machine gun and walked out against what he felt were the Germans. He shot the bark off of trees, smelled the sap exploded out of them by bullets. The machine gun got hot in his hands.

More images franked into his mind: a dead German, burned with white phosphorous, being eaten by a dog. A flattened US soldier beneath a car.

He thought about Miss Mary. He no longer wanted to die. He wanted to live with her in peace.

Fear replaced the determination to be killed.

The narrator told him, *All fear is the fear of losing something. It seems now that you want to live.*

He wanted to go home. He wanted Miss Mary to come with him. He felt the urge, for the first time in years, to pray.

He wanted to see his boys.

He got out of the forest. He was with Capa and his friend Buck Lanham in a jeep, the three heading to Paris. He heard a noise he recognised. It reminded him of Spain.

'Get out the car,' he yelled. 'Now!'

They jumped out, they rolled into a ditch. A Spanish plane, repurposed for this war, came at them. Its machine guns ripped into the jeep. It flew away. They listened to the ticking of its motor fade as it disappeared. Hemingway took one of his flasks – one schnapps, the other whiskey – and opened it. He stuck the neck of the flask in the corner of his mouth and drew the liquid deeply. He handed the flask to Capa, then to Lanham.

'We are done here,' he said. 'I am done here.'

He went back to Cuba. He waited, wanting, for Miss Mary to

come be with him. She tentatively agreed. The black dog came after him. Cuba was too peaceful. He hated it. He lacked a higher cause. He felt mortal again.

He did not write. The words were stuck in him like a wooden shard that he could not pull out. The drinking became deeper and harder.

Miss Mary came to see him. He tried to stem the drinking. She threatened to leave. He begged for forgiveness. They would fuck to draw lines beneath everything. She agreed to stay. She said she would marry him. They would start that family.

He sat with her one night at the Finca Vigía. They were naked beside the pool. The air was warm, the night sky darkening. He was reading an article about the war. He began to cry. He felt his tears fall on the page.

She looked over, but she said nothing for the longest time. 'What is it, Papa?' she asked eventually.

'Hürtgen.'

She nodded. She knew. She had come afterwards, had heard all the stories. Eighty-thousand dead men, left in shreds and ribbons amongst the trees. 'And what of it?'

'I was afraid,' he said. 'I was alive again, but I was scared.' He looked at her with his wet eyes. He brought up his fingers and pulled away his tears. 'I was scared.'

She understood.

He divorced Gellhorn in 1946. He never spoke to her again. He waited while Miss Mary divorced her husband. He rejoiced that they would finally be together.

He married Miss Mary. She became Wife #4.

He was nearly fifty and wanted another family. They tried.

Miss Mary found out she was pregnant in the middle of 1946.

They were happy. He considered stopping drinking. The thoughts still ran in his head. He still wanted a daughter. They would call this one 'Bridget'.

They decided on a trip to Idaho, and they arranged to meet his sons there. Bumby was a man now, home from Germany, safe again, and he took with him in his car Patrick and Gig. The thoughts running in their father's head made him imagine his boys broken and smashed along a road.

Hemingway loved Idaho. He had been invited there years before by the publicity office of a small town called Ketchum, and he went each year to shoot and to fish. He wanted Miss Mary to see the hills and the fields.

It was in Casper, Wyoming, that his world turned again. It was a cheap motel, set off the highway, and he and Miss Mary had turned into it late the night before, he grumbling and carrying their bags from their vehicle into the cabin.

But then it was morning and time to move again when she collapsed to the floor as he packed the car, and she began to shake and to scream. She held her side and curled up, and she went pale.

'Papa,' she said, trembling. 'Papa!'

The doctors in the hospital opened her up and they saw that the pregnancy was in the wrong place and that her fallopian tube had burst, and she was bleeding so heavily that she was going to die. And so her husband, the big bear of a man, stood beside her bed and said, 'No, keep going. Find another vein.'

They did, and Hemingway stood beside her with a bag of blood that he massaged as it was infused into her veins and a day later, she had turned the corner and would survive – but without the daughter that he had always craved.

The doctors told them they would have no children. They would have only each other to hitch their wagons to.

Hemingway walked out, once Miss Mary was asleep, into the streets of Casper, and he gazed up at the sky.

For once in his life, the narrator did not come to him. Nothing came to him that night, under the cold stillness of the Wyoming air, so after a while he went out and he left the hospital, and he walked back in the rain to the hotel.

# 9

# THE HUNTING SEASON
# IN VENICE (1948)

**I**t was late in the year, and cold outside, and Winston Churchill was sat on a wooden bench in the steam room of Venice's Hotel Gritti. He had a rotten cold that he had almost given up on trying to shift but Clemmy, his dear wife, had shooed him from his bed that morning and told him, for the love of God, to at least sit in the steam room for some time in order to try to loosen something.

He coughed and felt the great, wet mass move, then settle again in his chest like an elevator that began its ascent a split second before the power in the building shut down. Then he coughed again, and he felt and tasted its acidic burr. Still, it refused to shift.

Sweat dripped down his nose. He wiped it away, and he wondered what it was that she would have him do this morning. There was a lunch with the town's mayor that he could not get out of and, after that, he hoped to spend some time at the Gallerie dell'Accademia before, if he could, getting down to the edges of the canal, where the smell of the water mixed with the stone of the buildings, so that he could do what he had come to Italy to do: paint.

Now that he was no longer Prime Minister, he had been writing

157

his memoirs of the war years. That was something that he enjoyed. The first volume, *The Gathering Storm*, was out, with the second, *Their Finest Hour*, to follow early the next year. He figured that there would be five or six volumes in the end, a project that would take the best part of a decade. There were the speeches, too, and the essays. And all that was good, because the thought of having nothing to say or offer pierced his chest.

At least, he reasoned, he had his cigars and his paintings.

He sniffed and coughed once more, and he blinked the sweat from his eyes. He reached up and dragged his hand across the smooth pate of his head, and he looked at the droplets now dotting the webbing of his fingers. Then he coughed once again, for good measure, and wondered how many of those expulsions were due to the cigars and how many of them were due to this cold that had been racking him for the best part of a week and now seemed settled for the long term in his chest.

Eventually, Churchill left the steam room and put on a robe before walking back through the hotel to his rooms. He was supposed to dress within the confines of the steam room, but he hated the heat of his skin immediately afterwards and being clad quickly again in thick cotton made him sweat, so he put on the robe, shoved his feet into leather slippers and began to shuffle as quickly as he could back to his rooms.

He was moving down the corridors when he heard two voices coming towards him. One was thick, heavy and Russian, the accent strangling the English words before they were thrown out into the world. The other, which was all sighs and assertions, had a droning quality like that of a plane engine winding down before landing. Churchill's eyes were no longer what they were, so he did not recognise the larger of the forms until he came close, and then he realised it was Orson Welles.

Welles and his companion, a small and ridiculous-looking fat man, stopped and stared at Churchill. And Churchill, knowing only who Welles was from a brief meeting in London some years before, stopped and nodded at the tall American.

'Mr Welles,' he said, then Churchill, thinking about the lunch and the gallery and the prospect of some painting, carried on shuffling back to his room.

The end of 1948 was a strange juncture in the life of Orson Welles, and it followed eight tumultuous years. He had made it into Holly-wood with *Citizen Kane*, which he acknowledged as both the best and worst thing to happen to his career. It had been the best in that he had had total freedom to produce what he wanted – and which he did. And it was the worst in that, having everything at his disposal and complete freedom, the whole affair marked an apex in his life.

'I started at the top,' he would tell everyone who asked, 'and from there, I worked my way down.'

After *Kane*, there was *Ambersons*, but the studio had taken that one and re-cut it until it no longer felt like his, and so he went back on the stage and acted in other people's films. It was some time before he was given the train set back to play with. So he had made *The Stranger*, with Edward G. Robinson, and *The Lady from Shang-hai*. Now, he had a version of *Macbeth* that was sinking, despite the plaudits of most of the critics.

He had made *The Lady from Shanghai* with Rita Hayworth, his Wife #2, and she was the one that he now hated to think about. She was still his dear, sweet Rita, mother to their Rebecca. And he missed her; she was the second of his divorces in those eight years, and the one that pained him still the most. He and Virginia had

barely spoken since she had moved to South Africa and taken with her their daughter Christopher. And now Rebecca was in Los Angeles with her mother, and here he was, in Europe, making films for anyone that would have him as he tried to keep the funding together for *Othello*, even as it increasingly resembled a pearl necklace with a broken string, and he was having to catch each pearl in one hand while trying to maintain the necklace's formation with the other.

He was thirty-three, and he was broke, and he missed his daughters. He missed a family life, too, even if he had never been particularly good at it. It had been one of the things he had always wanted, to replace the fractured family of his youth. One part of that dream was to have a son who he could educate.

He was also aware that the rumours surrounding his departure from the US were following him like a miasma. 'No, I have not given up on Hollywood,' he would tell those who asked, while thinking, *But I do think it has given up on me.* There had been the too-late realisation that that town only loved you when you were successful and was quick to disavow you when you were not.

And so he had got out, although he wondered about the precise nature of the rumours. *I would have enjoyed listening to them, too,* he thought. There were so many things. The papers had been obsessed with an actress who had been murdered quite brutally just before he left, and he was pretty sure some loon might also put him in the frame for that.

And, now, through a set of circumstances that even he could barely make a clear direction of, he was in Italy where he had needed little persuasion to meet this Kossimoff, a Russian with something of the night about him, who was interested in dispersing his money somehow, and for some dark reason, away from Moscow.

The pair of them were eating breakfast at the Hotel Gritti, which

was the throw of a stone away from the main canal, and the meeting had so far not gone well, with Kossimoff asking too many questions about the movie stars of America and whether they would be in this film, and Welles had given up on trying to explain to him the importance of a cinematic *Othello* like his own and began to nod politely, letting this crazy Russian believe that, yes, Jimmy Cagney might be interested in playing the role of Iago.

'You have to understand, Mr Orson,' Kossimoff said, 'that it is important to me that you can make *more* money with this film. I do not want to give you what I have just so you can make your picture. I would like that money to come back to me – with *more* – and soon, too.'

Welles buttered some bread. 'I understand,' he said, nodding at the Russian. 'Now, making movies is a tricky business, so it is hard to guarantee anything without a finished picture in hand. I'm sure this is something you already know.'

Kossimoff waved his hand. The pair had been sparring in this manner for two days. Welles had noted in that time how the Russian's breakfasts always remained untouched, the short and fat man choosing to only drink one small cup of coffee after another.

*Remarkable*, Welles thought, *how he maintains such a girth with so little appetite.*

'You see, Mr Orson,' Kossimoff said. 'I am not a true Russian. I am half of an Armenian, so I do not have their appetite for penury. I will explain another way if you don't understand – I am a *white* Russian, not one of those *Red* Russians who merely pretends that he loves being poor while also pretending to hate money.'

'Right.'

'I like money, Mr Orson.' Kossimoff sat back and folded his arms over his ample stomach. The buttons on his waistcoat began to

strain. Welles could see the white of his shirt began to poke under the hem.

'Well, there could be lots of money with my *Othello* if we do it right,' Welles said. He looked into the impassive eyes of Kossimoff and saw the gaze of a man who had already made a decision, the outcome of which was of no interest to him.

Kossimoff leaned over, picked up his coffee and took a small, halting sip from it, then sat quietly.

Welles leaned forwards, too, and took his coffee and sipped from it. He felt its burned, acidic taste and knew it would reap hell on his delicate stomach.

'I think we should talk more about this in the next few days,' said Kossimoff. 'I'm going to be here in Venice for a while for some meetings. I'm sure that we can speak more. Maybe you can tell me something about Miss Hayworth? Something *secret*? You were married to her, no?'

'No. I mean, yes, I was. But she has no secrets, I'm afraid.'

Kossimoff looked disappointed. 'Very well,' he said. 'Now, I must go.'

'Let me walk with you to your rooms. I believe we're on the same floor.'

Welles walked with Kossimoff through the corridors of their hotel and towards their rooms. He felt as if the meeting had been a waste of time and that he should go back to Rome as soon as he could and get to reading the script for that Carol Reed picture that wanted him for its villain.

As Welles and Kossimoff rounded the corner, a short and wide man with the proportions of a toad came shuffling towards them in a thick, burgundy bathrobe and leather slippers. It took neither Welles nor Kossimoff more than a split second to realise that it was

Winston Churchill, looking strangely naked with his bare and thin ankles and without a cigar in his mouth.

Churchill looked up as he approached and saw Welles. A tremor of recognition started at the Englishman's ears when he and Welles made eye contact. Churchill nodded. 'Mr Welles,' he said, his head dipping slightly, without any interruption of his shuffling down the corridor.

Once around the corner and out of the hearing of Churchill, Kossimoff stopped and turned, putting his hand on Welles's jacket lapel. His face had widened and lifted, and there was a dazed brightness in his eyes.

'You know Mr Churchill?' he asked, his voice splashed with amazement. Welles had not imagined Kossimoff capable of excitement.

'Well, I...' The truth was that Welles and the former politician were barely acquainted apart from a brief conversation over the merits of Macbeth as a husband, an exchange that had occurred some six or seven years before. 'The truth is that Winston, dear Winny to those of us he's close to, has been a close friend of the Welles family ever since the turn of the century.'

Kossimoff clapped his hand to the top of his head and looked in the direction Churchill had gone. It was as if a blessing of unicorns had thundered by. 'Well, then, we need another meeting. You know a great man! I cannot believe my luck that you would know someone so influential as the man who saved Europe from those dreadful Germans!'

Ernest Hemingway was also staying at the Hotel Gritti, but he spent little time there and instead could be located most afternoons in the saloon of Harry's Bar.

Miss Mary was not with him. The couple had been in Italy for six months and had slowly driven up from the southern coast, past Rome and to Fossalta, where the old writer had received the wounds in his legs and knees that still haunted him. From there, they had gone to Cortina to ski before the main winter season, but Miss Mary had fallen and broken her ankle, ruining those plans and taking away his chance to sit and write in peace for some days. It was then, coming back to Venice, that an old friend from London who now lived in Tuscany had extended an invitation. So, with little exhortation, Hemingway had sent his wife off with a driver and was now spending his time writing at home in his hotel room, before wandering the small streets, alleyways and bridges that made up the city.

Hemingway had recently met a new family called the Ivanciches, who had been noble and rich but were now merely noble. Nobility, however, was still a form of currency by itself in Venice.

The Ivancich that Hemingway knew best was Gianfranco, who had been introduced to him by Nanuk Franchetti, who was in turn a friend of his Italian publishers. It was hard to remember, for a man of nearly fifty, how it had all come together. Hemingway had known for some time that relationships in Italy were complex and tricky, particularly around families, and had the tradition of spiralling quickly into delicious and strong complexities.

Now, he was waiting in Harry's Bar for Gianfranco, a young man who may still have been a boy. The air in the city was cool and damp, and the light was faded and grey, and Hemingway could smell the salt from the water of the canals.

The door to Harry's Bar opened, and he saw her for the first time. She came over the threshold with her head down, her hands holding together the collar of her coat. She looked around nervously. It

was obvious, immediately, to Hemingway that she spent little time in bars.

'Papa!' Gianfranco said, a little too loudly, as if introducing to friends a rare animal at the zoo. 'This is my sister Adriana.'

Hemingway rose to his feet and put out his hand. 'I'm Ernest,' he said, 'but you must, *may*, call me "Papa".'

She took his hand and he felt her delicate fingers slide across his palm. 'Adriana, sir.'

Hemingway motioned for them to sit down. 'Please.'

They sat, and Hemingway called over the waiter and ordered for them. Gianfranco turned to Adriana, 'See, I told you this was Ernest Hemingway.'

Adriana smiled, shyly. *She's young*, his narrator told him. He guessed that she was maybe around the age of seventeen, older if she had had a cloistered education somewhere. Hemingway suspected this was the case. She was tall, only an inch or so below his own height, and slim with dark hair that was cut to her shoulders. Her hair, he noticed, was wet, and he saw some water fall from it onto the shoulder of her dress. She caused him to think of a hummingbird.

'You came here, quickly, in the rain?' Hemingway asked.

'I did.'

She was unimaginably lovely to him, and he saw the brown of her eyes, the skin around them unmarked and unwrinkled. He looked at her shy smile and thought of how her forehead might crease with a joke, and he wanted nothing more than to spend as much time with her as he could so that he could make her laugh for ever. 'Your hair,' he said, with a nod of his head. 'You were rained upon.'

'I was.'

He reached into his pocket and took out his comb, then snapped it into two. 'Take this,' he said, handing over half, its edge jagged.

Adriana took the comb and looked at it, then took it and pushed it a few times through her hair to smooth it out. 'Thank you,' she said.

'May I offer you some whiskey for the cold?'

'No, thank you, Papa,' Adriana said. 'I don't drink.'

'Very well.'

He and Gianfranco began to talk about the duck hunting and of how they would go one day soon to the Marano Lagoon when the shooting season started. Adriana became quiet, listening to her brother speak English to this burly man she knew only from the newspapers, who spoke in an accent she found hard to understand.

Later, when it was time for Gianfranco and Adriana to leave, Hemingway stood, took hold of Adriana's hands and kissed them. 'If you would let me,' he said, 'I would like to call you "daughter".'

She nodded, unsure. She smiled. 'You may, Papa.'

'Very well, daughter. And, tomorrow, may I ask that you join me at my hotel, the Gritti, for lunch?' He looked at Gianfranco, as if remembering something. 'You may come, too,' he said, 'if you feel that you must.'

Gianfranco smiled. 'No, Papa,' he said. 'I am afraid I have some business tomorrow that I must attend to, but I am sure Adriana may accompany you by herself.'

Adriana smiled. Hemingway saw a blush rise in her cheeks, and he saw that hers was a beautiful smile that she kept as hidden as the sweetest secret. 'Tomorrow?' he asked, as if it were already set in stone and all she had to do was observe it.

'Tomorrow, Papa,' she said.

Hemingway nodded, and for a second, he felt his age hang on him like a well-cut, tailored suit. He felt older and worldly, like a gentleman fully come into himself. And a good part of it, he felt,

maybe even all of it, was the alluring, young Italian woman who had just entered his life.

Winston Churchill expected that he would see Orson Welles again. There was no great plan or no objective to their meetings at the Hotel Gritti in Venice, other than that they were staying at the same place and had something of a passing acquaintanceship. Churchill had seen Welles perform in *The Stranger* and knew he was of some renown also on the stage. They also had mutual friends within the American Army high command. That was about all of it, and his acknowledgement to the young director and actor was the same that one would give in the street if a person passing by had also known a friend of his.

So it was with some surprise that Welles made his way directly to Churchill's table the day after their passing in the hallway to speak. The tall American, who was beginning to carry some heft around his waist, stopped and ran his hand through his hair, then bowed stiffly. He looked like a boy called before the headmaster for an unknown reason.

'Mr Churchill, I am sorry to interrupt,' said Welles, his voice skipping a little. He coughed. 'Mr Churchill, I want to thank you for a great thing that you did for me yesterday.'

Churchill pointed to Clemmy's seat, now vacated. Her teacup was still in place, with some of the tea sitting at the bottom. 'Please sit down and take a seat,' he said.

'Oh, I couldn't.'

'That's perfectly fine. A rifleman would find it harder to reach you if you were not standing in a room full of people sat in chairs.'

'Thank you.'

'My people told me that during the war, when the world was

putting itself through those great agonies. *The one that stands tallest is the one that gets shot first*, they always told me. I had no reason to disbelieve them.' Churchill took out a cigar and laid it on the table. 'They very much do not like me smoking these in here,' he said, 'and I think it's something to do with these beautifully white walls. However, I am Winston Churchill, and it would be remiss if I were not smoking a cigar. I believe you like these, too?'

'I do.'

'Well, I'm not going to smoke this here, but I would like to smoke this soon.'

Welles read the meaning behind the words. 'I just wanted to thank you for yesterday, for your little nod in the corridor. That helped me out a lot.'

'How so? Was it something to do with that peculiar man you were with?'

Welles nodded. 'He's a financier, hopefully, for my next film. He has been a hard one to persuade, but he was impacted by the fact that I know you. Or, at the least, that he thinks you know me. I believe now that I have my funding, thanks to you, for my next project.'

'Ah… So that is it.'

'It is.'

'And what film are you making? Is it something that I would know? Something in the same vein of *The Stranger*? I liked that one.'

'No, I'm afraid not. A little more historic, perhaps. We're – I'm – doing a traditional version of *Othello*. We're just waiting and looking for the money to come through.'

'Set in this very city. Are you looking to play the title role yourself?'

'I am.'

'*Little shall I grace my cause in speaking for myself. Yet, by your*

*gracious patience, I will a round unvarnished tale deliver.* I believe that is one of the lines you cut for your stage version in New York, if I remember correctly?'

Welles smiled. 'That, sir, is correct.'

'It is a good line,' Churchill said, then picked up the cigar as he stood. 'Now, if you excuse me, Mr Welles, I will take my leave and smoke this on the way back to my rooms.'

Hemingway, in the following two weeks, felt more alive than he had felt in years. It was as if something long dormant had reawoken in him, and he felt the flutters in his chest of a new love affair, even if it remained a chaste one.

Miss Mary wrote to him most days and he responded to her lengthy letters about her stay in Tuscany to tell her that he was writing again and seeing something of the city. He did not mention Adriana.

He was writing, and it was the first time that he had set something down on paper since they had left the Finca Vigía to come to Europe. He rose, as he always did, in the morning when the air was at its coolest and he stayed in his hotel room, dressed in his robe, and sat at the desk that he had asked the staff to bring, and he began to write. He wrote about Venice and the old soldier who had come to die by its waters and the love that soldier felt for the young, Italian woman who could show him that last burst of passion.

After he had finished writing, Hemingway would telephone Adriana at her mother's house outside of the city, and he would tell her of what he had done this morning, why he had chosen that form and where he imagined that the story would carry him. And then he would insist that she join him for lunch, to which she would always agree, and they would set a time that each would leave, and they would meet somewhere around halfway along their route.

Italian tongues were starting to move about the pair. He had been married four times and she was nineteen and barely a woman, but he cared little about the implications on her reputation. He was happy for the first moments since the end of the war. The last time he had felt like this had been within the shadows of the Blitz and in the liberation of Paris, when he and Miss Mary had come together. After the Italian nurse, and the war reporter whose name he still refused to say out loud, and Miss Mary, war and love were to him two sides of the same coin.

'I have the easy feeling, daughter,' Hemingway said one afternoon as they strolled through the streets to their chosen cafe near St Mark's Square, 'that your mother does not approve of this.'

Adriana looked away. 'She is of the old Italian way,' she said. 'She worries that I will never find a husband.'

Hemingway tried to laugh, but it came out as a snort. 'I think you should find no problems there, daughter.'

'Oh, Papa,' she said. 'You do not know Venice. Or Italian.'

'I know Italian. And I saved this city during the war.'

Adriana put her hand on his arm. Hemingway felt the light pressure of her fingers through the fabric of his jacket. His heart fluttered. He tapped his fingers on top of hers and withdrew from her.

'*Venezia essere cuore italia, e mio cuore batte qui come nessun posto altro,*' he said.

Adriana laughed, and Hemingway loved its blossoming sound. He did not care that she was laughing at him. 'Oh, Papa,' she said. 'You speak Italian like a man who works with his hands.'

'How so?'

'"Venice is the heart of Italy, and my heart beats here like it does in no other place"? You are meant to say it as, *Venezia è il cuore palpitante dell'italia, e qui, come in nessun altro posto, trepida il mio.*

Right now, you sound like someone who has learned Italian only from a book.'

Hemingway laughed. 'You make me feel young again, daughter,' he said and looked at her.

Adriana walked on. 'Oh, Papa,' she said, then went quiet.

Hemingway walked a little faster to stay with her. 'Tell me something,' he said. 'Tell me anything. Who was your father?'

Adriana walked. 'He was murdered just after the war,' she said. 'And my brother found him. That is all there is to it.'

'I shall avenge him.'

'Don't be silly.'

'Do you miss him?'

'All children miss a father who is not there.'

Hemingway thought of his boys, now so distant to him. He stopped at a jewellery store. He beckoned Adriana to its window. 'What do you think?' he asked, pointing to all the necklaces and rings. 'Whatever you want, I'll buy for you, daughter.'

She shook her head, and he saw the blush rise once more in her cheeks. 'No, Papa,' she answered, as she turned and walked away.

One day, Hemingway and Adriana met at Al Todaro, their chosen cafe near St Mark's Square. He had been writing in the morning, and he had called her twice so that she knew where to meet him. The air outside was damp and the temperature of the wind was getting colder, and he could see, each morning, the thin ice forming on the surface of the canals that would need to be cracked.

He got there first, and he ordered and went outside, wrapped in his large and warm coat, wearing a hat. He felt the cold air bite at his ears and pinch at his nose, and the sun was bright and shone upon the water, but such things did not bother him. The cafe was to the

side of the canal in the plaza where Giardini Ex Reali met the Riva degli Schiavoni, and he could look from the tables outside across the waters to the church on San Giorgio Maggiore.

Hemingway thought of the book he was writing about an old soldier revitalised by love in Venice, and he knew without reservation that the young woman in it, his Renata, was really Adriana. And he thought that Adriana would be flattered, *should* be flattered, by his attentions, because what better objective of love was there than to write about somebody?

The waiter came and put two drinks, along with the bill, onto the table, smiled at the old writer and moved away. He knew, without introduction, who Hemingway was.

Hemingway's feet were cold in his shoes, and he stamped them lightly against the stone floor. Winter was coming, and he knew that he would soon need his thick boots. He readjusted his thick scarf once more and brought together the collar of his coat, and he rubbed his hands.

'What is this?'

Hemingway turned in his seat and saw Adriana. She pointed at the small table between the two chairs he had taken for them, and the deep-red, iced drinks on it.

'They're what we call Bloody Marys,' he said.

Adriana sat. 'I've never had one.'

Hemingway smiled. 'That's why I've got one for you, daughter. So I can say that I bought you your first drink.'

Adriana looked around. 'People will talk.'

He jammed his hands into the pockets of his coat. 'People always talk about me,' he said.

'They will talk about me, drinking alcohol with a married man. This is Venice.'

He nodded. 'Well, I wouldn't want to bring shame on you, daughter.'

Adriana smiled. She took the drink and sipped from it. She tasted the acid of the tomato juice and the spices mixed into it. Her tongue noted the slight warmth from what she assumed was the alcohol. She put down the glass. 'Do you drink many of these?' she asked.

Hemingway nodded. He drank too much of them, his doctors said. He drank too much, Miss Mary said. He told them that he drank all that he wanted to drink. He leaned into Adriana. 'Few things have ever made me feel better,' he said. 'My idea of heaven is one where we all drink ourselves to death – but we cannot die!' He sat back again, with a smile on his face like that of a child eager for their weak joke to be laughed at.

Adriana sipped once more at the drink. 'I don't know if I can drink much more of this,' she said, putting it down.

Hemingway slipped his hand from his pocket, reached over the table and put it on hers. Adriana startled and pulled hers a small distance away. 'Your skin is cold,' she said. 'Where are your gloves?'

'I don't need them.' He put his hand back over hers. 'My marriage is...' he said and let the rest of the sentence pass into the air. 'I have felt empty until I came here.'

'Papa...' Adriana pulled her hand away, further, for a second time. Hemingway moved his hand closer on the arm of her chair, bunched together in a fist, then he opened his fingers slightly, extended the smallest of them and stroked with it the side of her hand. He then tapped the end of each finger, one by one, and moved down them, from largest to smallest, as if running his hand along the keys of a piano.

'Your hand.' He caressed the skin on her knuckles. 'This is something for me to remember you by.'

Adriana said nothing.

'I am writing better', he continued, 'than ever before, and it is because of you, daughter. You are in my new one, and it is bigger than everything before. And your brother is in it, too, and his friends, and it is about being here in Venice.'

Later that afternoon, Hemingway and Adriana went back to the Hotel Gritti, from where they got onto a gondola. The head waiter from the hotel came out with a bottle of whiskey and some glasses, and Hemingway and Adriana sat in the cabin, where he closed them off from the world.

Adriana was young, and as Hemingway sat down, she leaned over and kissed him briefly on the lips, then sat back. She smiled and laughed, and it was the beautiful and girlish peal of a young woman discovering something new and undetected about herself.

'I'm sorry, Papa,' she said. 'It was a mistake.' She took the whiskey and poured a little of it into a glass, then drank it. Hemingway thought that she had aged so much in just that hour or so from that Bloody Mary.

'I hope there are many more mistakes like that,' he said.

The driver took the boat down towards the Accademia and then towards the canal by Campo San Barnaba, then headed back onto the Grand Canal. Adriana slipped her hand inside Hemingway's, and she felt the warmth of his palm just beyond the coldness of his fingers.

She leaned her head upon his shoulder, and he felt her hair brush up against his nose.

'May I ask something, Papa? A favour?'

'Of course, daughter.' Hemingway gently breathed in the scent of her hair.

'My brother', she said, drowsily, the whiskey going into her blood, 'is back in town next week, and he would like you to come shooting with us. There is a Russian coming along that he wants to impress.'

Orson Welles had spent more time with the same Russian than he had wanted to, but the promise of funding was still further than he could reach. This troubled him greatly, as it would mean more time spent in hotels with various dubious figures of foreign origin, all of them calculating how they could funnel their money into his productions and, most importantly, how they could funnel even more money back out of them.

Now, Kossimoff was telling him that he was only in Venice for two more days, after which he was headed back to Geneva, where he lived in some kind of gilded exile, so this final breakfast was the last time they could meet for some months. Besides, Kossimoff said he had business with other people before he left, so he was really doing him a favour. He had also begun to needle for two things – some intimate details of Rita Hayworth, which Welles had decided firmly to himself that he was not going to give, and an introduction to Churchill.

Welles arrived first in the restaurant of the Hotel Gritti and sat to wait. He was sure that the Russian knew this and was delaying his own entrance in response. A waitress came over for his order, and Welles asked just for a glass of grapefruit juice. If anything, he believed he might have to lose weight if he was going to do that thing in Vienna with Carol Reed.

The last few years had been tough and the fall had been hard. Actor for hire now, occasional hopeful director. Two divorces, too, a child in each one, now living with their mothers, both of them barely seen. He was becoming his own father rather than the one he had hoped to be.

Kossimoff arrived and sat down. The Russian looked as if he had been drinking the night before and, possibly, that morning, too. His eyes were rimmed with red and his shirt collar was too tight around his neck, causing his face to pinken. Kossimoff coughed, and the scent of something alcoholic entered the breakfast rooms.

'Good morning, Mr Orson,' Kossimoff said, plucking at his waist-coat and shirt. He coughed again. 'Do you think they have coffee?'

'I do,' said Welles. He signalled and asked for some to be brought over. It arrived within seconds.

'Do you want to talk more about the film?' Kossimoff said, after taking two mouthfuls of the hot coffee. He looked over at Welles.

The abruptness of the question should not have surprised Welles, but it still did, and he found himself without an answer.

'I have a bid for you, instead,' said Kossimoff. 'I am meeting some Italians here tomorrow to go hunting for ducks. They are all busi-nessmen, or they want to be, and they are bringing on their trip this Mr Ernest Hemingway. I think you know him.'

Welles thought back to the project room in 1937 in New York. He smiled.

Kossimoff picked up on the smile. 'I see. Well, he is their guest tomorrow and I think that you two should talk a little about maybe making a picture from one of his works. He writes, you direct.'

'Oh, I don't think that will work.'

'Very well.'

The door to the restaurant opened, and Churchill walked in, waving away a waiter who tried to guide him to a corner table. The former Prime Minister looked around, saw Welles and Kossimoff, and began walking in their direction. Without saying anything, he stopped at their table, looked Welles in the eye, glanced at Kossimoff,

then went into the deepest bow that he could. Welles stood up and bowed back.

Churchill put his arms around Welles in a deep embrace. 'My dear Orson,' he said. 'My old friend.' He looked at Kossimoff. 'Good morning to you.' Stepping back, Churchill winked, clapped his hand on Welles's shoulder and began to shuffle off once again through the restaurant.

Welles turned back to Kossimoff. He raised his eyebrows and nodded backwards in the direction of Churchill.

The Russian sat with his mouth open. 'Whatever happens tomorrow at the hunting,' he said, 'I will give you the money for your *Othello*.'

It was early in the morning and still dark when the boats went out onto the lagoons, and the boatmen pushing them along had to break the ice in front of them. It had been so cold that some thought that they might need to burn paraffin on the surface in order to weaken it.

But, eventually, the paraffin was not needed and so they slid slowly through the water, cutting through the thin ice, towards the blinds from which they would shoot the ducks.

They had all met outside Venice in a hunting lodge belonging to a friend of the Ivanciches and, after coffee and brandy to warm their blood, had gone back outside to the cars and were driven down to the jetties, then launched in boats into the water.

Ernest Hemingway sat at the front of his boat, where he took an oar and turned it upside down to crack the ice. 'Don't worry,' he told his poler, who he sensed resented him, 'I am a boatman, too.'

He knew Adriana was out there, also in one of the boats, and

it was her first time shooting ducks, and he hoped that she would shoot well and true. And he hoped, too, to see again the nape of her neck beneath the hair he would hate to see her cut short.

Eventually, the boat ran up against the sand and the silt, and Hemingway stepped over its side.

'To the left,' said the boatman. 'Your barrel is there. There will be more to join you soon.'

Hemingway nodded and moved in the direction pointed to him. His feet crunched on the ice formed in the sand, and he saw the morning's early mist rise in front of him. Frozen grass broke beneath his feet.

He saw the barrel then, lying in the ground like the torso of a bull after the fight. He went over to it, carrying his guns, and he sat and counted quickly the shells left for him and the small box of food and wine. And when he had checked everything in the box, he relaxed a little and was happy.

It was about an hour that he sat there until the boatman came back, and he saw the taller figure with him and he recognised, despite the whispering, the voice like a deep note held too long on a church organ.

'Papa,' the voice said, and Hemingway knew it was Welles. 'We meet again.'

'Hi, Orson,' Hemingway said in a low voice, and then he smiled. 'It's good to see you again. How long has it been?'

'Too long. It's good to see you.' Welles crouched down into the adjoining barrel and looked out at the marshes. There was little for his eyes to see. 'Tell me,' he said. 'What am I looking for?'

'Ducks.'

'I see.' He looked over at Hemingway and saw the beginnings of sag and heft in his jowls, and of his movements that seemed stiff,

and how his legs looked thin beneath the bulk of his body. It was only his hands that looked strong.

The boatman, who was about eight feet away, stamped his feet and clapped his hands as if to warm them. There was a fluttering on the marshes.

'They hate us,' Hemingway said. 'We are rich Americans who are doing for fun what they think *they* should be doing. So he's fucking with the ducks to ruin our day.'

Welles rubbed his own hands together. 'It's mighty cold,' he said. 'It is.'

There was a long, rasping call of a wooden pipe being blown heavily upon, and a few score of ducks went into the air. Hemingway raised his gun and shot once, then twice. Some shapes fell to the ground and Welles saw one of the party's dogs gallop over, pick whatever it was up and then run back to the boat.

'I got one,' said Hemingway. 'Possibly two.'

The dog turned and ran into the marsh once again, stopped and picked up what was on the ground, then came back.

'Definitely two,' said Welles.

'That's good.' Hemingway racked the shotgun and put another shell in it. He looked over to Welles. 'You have no gun?' he questioned. 'Do you not shoot?'

Hemingway put his gun on the ground, reached into his barrel and took out the second weapon. 'You want this, old stick?' he asked Welles. 'I brought a couple.'

'No. I remember my father.'

'Your father?'

'Yes. He was an avid hunter. And then one day, he got rid of all his guns, and he just said, "I've killed enough animals, and I'm ashamed of myself." I've always remembered that of him.'

Hemingway took back the gun. 'You sound like you loved him.'

'Every boy should love his father.'

Hemingway nodded. He thought of Clarence Hemingway. He thought of the anger he felt at him for choosing to leave him so early. 'I have three boys,' he said, eventually. 'Never thought that would happen. I thought I might have a daughter along the way. You?'

'Two girls.'

'You ever wanted a son?'

'Of course.'

Hemingway sighted his gun on the marshes, imagined the fluttering wings of the ducks as they would take off. He rested his finger on the trigger of the shotgun. 'My old man killed himself,' he said. 'Don't know why, but he took a gun one day and put it to his head, and he got himself out of here. I hated him for it, but now I imagine what an act of bravery it must have been for him to choose to go out at the full measure of his strength.'

'I don't see it like that.'

There was another whining call, and the ducks flew again. Hemingway shot twice, but nothing fell. 'Damn, I missed them,' he said.

It felt in the cold marsh that it was just the two of them, and Welles imagined for a moment that they were the only two people left on earth. It was a situation that invited the confessing of sins. 'My father never did anything after he was young,' he said. 'He had all this money, and he spent it on enjoying all the good things, but then he got to drink too much. So when I was a boy, I told him I wouldn't see him again until he stopped, because he was becoming an embarrassment. Can you imagine a boy saying such a thing like that to his father?'

Hemingway racked the shotgun again. 'And then what happened?' he asked.

'He died, before I ever saw him again. And, so, I was an orphan

at seventeen, and that's when I went back to Europe again. It seems that I always come here when things begin to go wrong.'

'The sacrifices of our youth, I reckon. I came here for the first time when I was seventeen, too. I took metal in my knee, and I lost friends. And I saved Venice.' Hemingway aimed. 'What brings you here now?'

'Money,' Welles said. 'I'm trying to raise it for an *Othello* I want to do, and I've been meeting this Russian here who has crazy money.' He pointed into the distance. 'He's over there somewhere. He invited me here to meet you, thought that maybe I could do a picture of one of your books or stories.'

Hemingway looked at Welles. 'There's always an angle with these people.' He aimed and fired the gun again. Once more, he hit nothing. 'Do you know why I'm here? I'm here on vacation with Miss Mary, but she went and broke her ankle, so I'm staying in Venice. And you know what else? I'm writing something new, and I think it's better than anything else I ever did before. And it's all about a girl I met here in Venice, nineteen years old and she's given me this great new shot at writing!'

'You sound like a man in love.'

Hemingway shook his head and shrugged. 'Damn! Those birds are flying well today.'

Welles looked over the dark lagoon, the sounds of shooting fading away in the gloaming light. He could smell the spent powder from the guns. 'When were you last in Spain?' he asked.

Hemingway shrugged. 'Oh, 1938,' he said. 'When the whole business was starting. Or put another way – too long ago now.'

'Some good fights over there in Spain this year.'

'That I've heard.'

Welles turned back to Hemingway. 'Did you know that Martha wrote about me for *LIFE*? Her review just about killed my *Macbeth*.'

Hemingway turned and his nostrils flared. 'I don't speak of her any more. She's been dead to me for the longest time. And I never read what she writes. Did she write *anything* good about you?'

Welles shook his head. 'No.'

Hemingway shrugged. '*The Spanish Earth* was her idea, you know? She didn't like your voice on it. And like a chump, I listened to her.'

'I figure she never liked me.'

'They never do. Malcolm Cowley just wrote about me for *LIFE*, too, and that little son of a bitch wrote all about the boating I did during the war, which has got the Cubans rattled about me. They're watching me now like I'm a bad spy. I wish these writers would let me die before they picked away at my bones.'

When the shooting was over and the boats were ready to go, the party met in the marshes by a small portable table where they lined up all the shot ducks to count them. Hemingway had shot poorly but not much worse than anyone else.

Adriana was there, awkwardly holding a gun. Her clothes were barely muddied.

Hemingway put his hand on Welles's shoulder, and he glanced over at Adriana. 'It is a fine thing to be in love without consummation,' he said.

Welles laughed. 'That sounds like someone doing their best to imitate you', he said, 'and doing it poorly.'

Hemingway laughed. 'Well, it needs a little more work, but I have always been my best editor.'

After taking his arm away from Welles's shoulder, Hemingway walked over to Adriana and asked her how she felt after her first shoot. 'How was it, daughter?' he asked.

She quoted Bismarck. 'People never lie so much as after a hunt, during a war or before an election.'

Hemingway laughed.

Someone amongst the group poured red wine into cups and handed one to each person. Welles drank his and felt his cheeks warm. He looked over to Hemingway, who had walked to a quiet spot by himself about fifteen feet from the group.

Gradually, everyone moved over to him. The large American put his hand in his pocket and took out two of the spent shells from the morning. 'I want to leave these here,' he said, going slowly and wearily down onto one knee. He took out a knife and carved away some of the wet, thick mud of the marsh, then placed into it the emptied shells and a 1,000-lira note. 'This is restitution,' he said, 'for what the Italians have given this old and injured soldier.'

The light was starting to come up. A clearness had formed on the lagoon that had not been apparent some hours before. It was still cold and there was still ice on the surface, but now it was time for everyone to return to Venice, where it would be warm.

Welles and Hemingway did not return on the same boats. Welles stayed with his Russian, who did not detect his fake smiles and shakes of his head, and Hemingway chose to go instead with the Ivanciches. They said goodbye, and it was a brief and sure thing, each clasping the other by the arm, and then they went to the boats, with their surly boatmen, and floated separately back to the shores. Hemingway went first, and Welles saw his bulk in the boat, talking to his poler, gradually moving further away and fading from view, until a thick curl of fog blew between them, and the writer, from that point, was entirely gone.

# TILTING AT WINDMILLS
# (1958)

**O**rson Welles was counting his failures. There were many of them. So far, it was two marriages, the films – *Citizen Kane*, *The Magnificent Ambersons*, *The Lady from Shanghai*, *Mr Arkadin* and now *Touch of Evil* – he had made and the films that had slipped away from him. He still wanted to make *Don Quixote*, which he called 'the Spanish film'.

He sat in a booth at the far end of the bar at the Musso & Frank Grill on Hollywood Boulevard, and he looked down at the book and the glass on his table. He was trying, in his forty-third year, to be grateful for the small mercies and sacraments of life.

At that moment, he was glad to not hear the damned zither music from *The Third Man*. The owners at the restaurant liked him and liked when he came in, and they knew instinctively not to have anyone play that music.

He began to think of the music: *Dum-dee-dum-dum-dum-DUM-DUM. Dum-dee-dum-dum-dum-DUM-DUM.*

There was that small, falling feeling of disappointment, the

younger cousin to the sense of failure as some new thing moved further into the distance.

It was the music again, and he had brought it on to himself. This time, it was inside his head. But someone else was playing it, usually, and when they did, his subconscious mind was always aware first, before his brain caught on and realised that he was hearing it *again*. Every bar, every club, every TV show, it seemed that he could not escape the shadow of *The Third Man*. It was more painful because he had taken a flat fee for it rather than a percentage of the box office and somehow managed in doing so to rob himself from his own pocket.

It had followed him from those sewers in Vienna to Rome and to Paris. He had even heard it the evening after he married in London for the third time. It came with him to New York, the cab driver humming it beneath his breath when taking Welles to the hospital to see his third daughter being born.

He had been hoping for a son, and it was a wish that he had no way of explaining, although he supposed some Austrian analyst might posit that he was seeking to take the place of his own addled father, building a family block by block, one idealised piece at a time. Getting back to what he had never had. That might have been the answer, but there were cellars and basements in his mind that he chose not to probe any further than necessary.

He closed his eyes and willed his mind not to play the tune. He listened to the chatter and the low conversations at the end of the bar. The music went. Life seemed normal once more, and he hoped to not think of the music again lest it reappear. Another small mercy.

He thought of Paola. They had married, of course, because she was pregnant, although he supposed they would have got there eventually. And she was beautiful, and she was dependable, and she

subverted her own career without complaint to support the tottering failure of his own. Beautiful Paola, with her long, thin nose and her square chin and thick eyebrows, all those features that slotted so seamlessly together like the jagged borders of countries on a map. She loved him unconditionally, but even she could see that he had become an international joke and the world's youngest has-been. A golden child who had skipped over success to become a failed adult.

He had changed along the way from being an actor and director who became something of a star to a star that mostly acted and, occasionally, directed. Respected and known but not particularly liked.

He was always reminded of it. Just now, some kid called Ed had swung by his table to say that he admired his work. Said he also made films. Seemed like a nice guy. Wide-eyed, wearing an angora sweater.

Everyone wanted to work for him, but no one wanted to employ him; friends at the bottom did not equal friends at the top. He was too difficult, it seemed, and he would probably agree with them – too many arguments, too much bad behaviour from a man who had been treating fools and hacks and journeymen with all the contempt that he felt fools and hacks and journeymen deserved.

It was the people at the top who always executed him. And it was happening again. The studio was understanding and tolerant. They had loved the dailies for *Touch of Evil*. But then, without warning, they replaced him – HIM – with a damned director of television cowboy shows and even the film's star could do little to protect him. Now, they were butchering the edit.

He drank his brandy and sucked down some smoke from his cigar. He mumbled to himself through the fogginess of his mind. 'A television director', he said, 'is someone who has not had the decency or dignity to give prostitution a chance first!'

Welles laughed to himself. A realisation. *I'm a hypocrite,* he thought. He was contracted to make a pilot for NBC called *The Fountain of Youth,* which would be the first of a run of one-off television dramas, all adaptations under his name. And if it worked, then there would be a whole series of them that would keep him afloat.

Welles drew once again on the cigar. He thought about ordering a steak, but he felt the pinch in his wallet. He looked down once more at the table and at the book. He flicked at its cover. *Don Quixote.*

'I miss Spain,' he said. The words had always been there, hidden. But now they had come out. He missed Spain because he had been there for some time but left after the *Mr Arkadin* business. Well, he called it *Mr Arkadin.* His former business partners now called it *Confidential Report.* It had been another one of his films taken from him by *them* – and it was always *them,* the faceless horde of talentless and money-obsessed studio hacks. Recut, released.

*These were not my films,* he thought. *They have only my name above their title. Directed by Orson Welles. Edited by committee. Released by vagabonds.*

It was like finding out one of your beloved children was now your nephew or a cousin whose name you could never remember.

Even theatre was dead. He was doing *King Lear* in New York when he slipped from the stage and sprained his ankle. Marlene Dietrich came to see him a few days later to talk about doing *The Sun Also Rises* on stage in London, and he turned to Paola and said, 'Look, it's the most beautiful woman in the world.' And then Paola had nudged him, a playful elbow in his side and he tottered, fell and broke the other ankle. *King Lear* was done, then, from a wheelchair. Dietrich turned and left, and the curtain for *The Sun Also Rises* never rose.

*Lear* was a disaster, the budget ballooning, the critics savaging it on opening. Twenty-six performances and then its capsizing, almost taking with it the entire theatre company.

Such headlines did nothing for his reputation.

The only good thing about it was to see once again Geraldine Fitzgerald's boy, now almost eighteen. Welles had loved Geraldine once nearly two decades ago when they were so much younger and the world was so much more open to them. Now, she was in his *Lear*, and her boy, this young, dark and heavy boy, had sat in the stalls during rehearsals and asked question upon question about cameras and blocking and actors. He sat with him often, and Welles wanted to reach his hand out and pat his arm. And Welles looked at him with his eyes and his dark hair and his hopes of directing, and he wondered.

He flicked once more at the cover of *Don Quixote*. He knew he had to pick it up and think of its adaptation, of moving the ancient story to modern-day Spain, placing its two characters out of place and out of time.

Welles sighed and thought glumly of the phrase 'out of time'.

*Time gone*, he thought. *Loves left; opportunities evaporated into the air. Things never to be reclaimed.*

'I have wasted it,' he said to himself, 'and now it wastes me.'

He ordered a steak and another brandy, and he waited for them to come. There was a feeling in his chest that he believed lesser men would call 'loneliness', a curious sensation for one who always felt so much at ease without others. He had possessed the ability from a young age to take or leave company as if he were stepping off a stage and going back into normal life. He did not, most times, notice the closing of the door as one wife or another left because he always still had for himself his arts and his tricks and his books.

His back ached a little more. It was harder than ever before to keep his weight down. There was grey in his hair. It seemed that he was both out of time and feeling it catch up with him.

America was changing. The world was changing. All the old things once thought permanent were moving away in time. He looked at these new players coming through and landing as he had twenty years before, and he hated them and their acting. Punks like this Brando and Dean and Clift who thought that they were becoming the characters and forgot that it was *acting*. And the whole thing with the mumbling and the histrionics and the slovenliness – that, Welles thought, was unbecoming.

He stubbed out the cigar. 'Amateurs,' he said, to no one in particular.

He looked at *Don Quixote* again.

'I am a man in the wrong century,' he said. 'And so are you, old friend.' He had loved the book for years, with its silly tales of an old madman who thought himself nobility and travelled around Spain, righting non-existent wrongs, tilting at windmills.

The steak came, and the brandy, and Welles began to eat and drink. He looked at the book in front of him, felt the lunacy of chasing a past that may never have existed.

*We are the same*, he thought.

He chewed, and he thought of *Don Quixote*, and he thought of Spain. He nodded to himself as if he knew he was about to realise something for the first time. Something that had always been there. An answer hidden by its own question.

He should go back and do the film as much as he could afford, and when he could allot the time to do it. And he should shoot until he knew he had shot enough. And it would be all his. Spain was the place to do that.

He thought of its heat and its food, of the waters that ran by its coast. He thought about the hills and the plains, of a horse that might gallop across them, a knight on its back. He thought of the horse, now a motorcycle, the knight old and demented, chasing a mirage of a past, determined to make it exist again. He thought of the dust in the air, and the smells in Seville around the bullring of lavender, and he imagined himself high up in its hills where the air was cool enough to be comfortable. It was Spain. Beautiful, old Spain, with its churches and its religion and its traditions. Red wine drunk in squares during the day, thick hams carved into thin slices in the evenings, conversations that went deep into the night. Already, the breath felt lighter in his chest.

That was the land of *Don Quixote*. His land, too. A place where he could make his work. To live and grow old and die upon its soils and sands.

'The answer is not in Spain,' he said, setting down his knife and his fork. 'The answer *is* Spain.'

# 11

# THE OLD MAN AND
# THE DESTITUTE KING
# (1958 TO 1959)

*'Orson is so much like a destitute king – not because he was
thrown away from the kingdom but because there is no
kingdom good enough for Orson Welles.'*
– JEANNE MOREAU

The revolutionaries came down from the mountains, day by day
and month by month. They came during the day, and they came
during the night, and sometimes they stole and sometimes they
killed. But mostly, they attacked the government of Cuba. And they
kept coming and coming, and the government tried each time to
push them back, but the revolutionaries still came.

Ernest Hemingway read the reports each morning, and his brain
tried each day to make sense of what they were doing. He had
begun to think he was Cuban. *Hell*, he thought, *I have lived here
long enough, and I love the Cubans and their government, and I love
this Castro, even if I don't know what it is that he is or what he wants
or when or how.*

He read the reports and some days he felt he was one with the rebels. On other days, he felt at one with the government. Spain had taught him that it was impossible to find purity on one side or the other.

And he thought of Spain now, of those nights in the Hotel Florida. He thought of his vulnerability, his naivete. And he thought of Dos Passos and the warnings he had given and of the warnings Hemingway had handed back. He knew how a patriot today could be a traitor tomorrow without a change in-between, and he suspected that there were things that a man had to do in difficult and serious war times.

If there was anything that Hemingway could be sure of, it was that Cuba was changing. The air was getting wound tighter and thicker as Fulgencio Batista and his government laboured to wipe out the revolutionaries, the atmosphere like a hand clenched across the throat. But the revolutionaries still came down from the mountains, and then they fanned out across the country and amongst the towns until no one was sure how many there were, where they really were, what they wanted or how they planned to behave once they had achieved their goal.

Hemingway had seen these rebels. They came to the Finca Vigía one afternoon. They were not looking for him but for another. They killed one of his dogs.

Fear pooled in his chest. He looked back to home, and he bought the house in Ketchum, so that he and Miss Mary could go there if they needed to. He looked at the house in the cold hills of Idaho, and he wondered how he would live there with Miss Mary, but he knew that the answer to that question was fate, and it was the answer that would find him, not he it.

The US ambassador came to the Finca Vigía, and he advised

Hemingway to leave. The US was beginning to pull out its people, he said. 'You should go, too,' he said.

'This is my home.'

'Very well, Papa,' the ambassador replied. Then he left the island.

Hemingway became alone in Cuba. He became lonely. He practised his suicide for others, showing them how he would put the gun on the floor, then his mouth over the barrel and his toe on the trigger. 'Bang!' he would say and laugh at their shocked faces.

The end, he felt, was coming. He was old now and cautious. His body was failing. He felt fragile. The doctors kept telling him not to drink, but he ignored them. He was impotent. Eyesight bad, too. Aches and pains, injuries.

If he had to put a pin on the map where it had all really started to go wrong, it was in Africa: two plane crashes within days of each other in Uganda. The first had been bad enough, the plane crashing into the bush, but he, Miss Mary and the pilot had stayed up all night, drinking, until a boat came. But then they got onto a second plane and that one had crashed, the doors jammed shut. And he was too big, unlike Miss Mary and the pilot, to climb out of the broken windows, so he lined his head up against the door and smashed it as hard and as much as he could until he got out while the flames burned his face and his arms. He nearly died then, and he knew that, and he also knew that he was never again the same man.

Miss Mary saw that, too. She still held the same love for him. She even held it when they fought. She held it when he turned and hit her. She did not fear her death at his hands. She understood him to be a towering, magnetic force; she could not leave him because of that.

She knew his injuries from the plane crashes: the broken skull, the breaks in his back, the burns. She helped him when his vision

swam and when it multiplied. She understood his confusion, and she repeated words back to him in the times when he could not hear her. She braced herself when the anger came from the headaches.

She was with him in Kenya, weeks after the crash, when they went to see Patrick. She saw the fights between them. She saw him berate his boy. She saw the boy leave. She knew inside that the boy and the father would never see one another again.

Miss Mary saw that Papa had lost his sons. She saw Gig, Son #3, lost to his own darkness. She was with her husband when the call came that the boy – now a man – had been arrested in Los Angeles, in a women's bathroom, wearing female clothes. She saw her husband, purple-faced, on the phone to Pauline, to Wife #2.

'It's your fault!' he screamed at Pauline. 'It's your fault he's like this! Why did you ever take him from me?'

Pauline died the next day from a burst tumour. Hemingway blamed his son. Gig blamed him.

Gig wrote, *You have destroyed so many of us.*

Miss Mary saw the Adriana girl when she came out to Cuba, and she saw Papa when he went back to write and came up with *The Old Man and the Sea.* She saw the fever he wrote it in. She saw the critics love it. She understood that it was a last burst of sun before the dark of the night. She held her breath.

Sweden called with THE BIG PRIZE. Papa did not go. He blamed his health.

He read his written answers when the TV people came for an interview. It was a staccato. His voice was high, nearly nasal. He struggled. It pained her to see it.

He stumbled. He hesitated. 'I am sorry', he said, 'that I will not be able to go to Sweden... on the orders of my doctor... who says that I am doing very well... after... the... serious... internal injuries

that I received in the air crashes... and that... he believes... that it would be... very bad for me to interrupt... the regime... which I have been... maintaining.'

He spoke about his books. He breathed heavily between his words. He spoke about his novels and his short stories. He lamented that one of the latter had turned into one of the former.

He sent a speech to Stockholm, where the US ambassador read it out for him.

He wrote:

> Writing, at its best, is a lonely life. Organisations for writers palliate the writer's loneliness but I doubt if they improve his writing. He grows in public stature as he sheds his loneliness and often his work deteriorates. For he does his work alone and if he is a good enough writer, he must face eternity, or the lack of it, each day.

He read the news reports later, in Havana. They were naked by the pool. His eyes were blank, and his mind was clouded.

'Miss Mary,' he said. There was a frozen daiquiri next to him, its ice melting in the warm air. His face shuddered. There was a tremble in his shoulder.

'Yes, Papa.' She saw him. She knew it was fear.

'I am finished,' he said. 'No one who ever won the Swedish thing ever wrote anything worth a lick afterwards.'

It was 1959, and the old man known as Ernest Hemingway still liked to rise early, when the air was at its coolest, go to his desk and write. But he just stared at the words now – a 40,000-word magazine assignment that he had somehow let tangle into more than 100,000 words. All those unwanted letters and syllables. Three

words produced for every word wanted. And he did not know in his addled mind how to cut any of them.

Hemingway looked at the words on the page and he read over the sentences in front of him, pencil in hand. And he would lean in to see because of his fading eyesight, the colours draining day by day from his eyes, everything moving out of focus, and he would try to judge on what he would have done thirty years ago when the words came and went with ease. And he knew somehow that that ability, which may have been given to him by God herself, had gone and would never come back.

'It's all just false and chickenshit,' he said, then stood up from his desk and walked barefoot out through the house and down to the pool.

It was so early that Miss Mary was still asleep, so he pulled the door gently towards him to close it and then walked down to the water.

He stripped down to his skin, and he smelled the lavender trees, and he thought of Spain, and he felt the day's budding heat in the air.

His mind had been emptied, like a room slowly being stripped of its furniture. It had been that way for some time, but now he felt at peace with it.

*Just chickenshit*, he thought. *Chickenshit and false.*

He stepped one foot into the pool and felt the cold water come over his toes and lap at his ankles. He put the other in. There were dead leaves in the water. He saw an insect skate across the surface, following the ripples his steps had made. He felt the need to piss.

He stepped back out of the pool and went and pissed in the trees, knowing no one could see him hesitate.

*Be brave*, he told himself. *This is the moment.*

He put both feet in the water now and stood naked in the light breeze. Then he stepped down again until the cold went up to his knees, then again to his waist, then again until his chest. Then he leaned forward and fell until the water was rolling all over him, and its coldness was upon his shoulders and his back.

He swam a few lengths and remembered, and he stopped and stood and looked back on his house with Miss Mary, and he knew it felt right that he should die here in Havana, where he had lived for so many years.

*This place of so many memories,* he thought. *OK, let's go.*

He put his head beneath the water and felt the coldness enter his ears. He realised he was holding his breath, and he let it go, and he watched the fat bubbles erupt to the surface like hydrogen clouds. There was no feeling at first, his lungs emptied of air and he felt somewhat at peace beneath the clean water.

*Not long to go,* he thought. *No more of this chickenshit.*

The body began to want air. He ignored it, told himself that it was time to go. His lungs began to spasm. He held tight.

*Go, go,* he said to himself.

His chest began to move and heave. He willed himself to stay. The heaves became more violent. They racked his torso. His body did not understand the mind.

The thoughts were of his boys, all now lost to him. They were of Miss Mary, still asleep in the house. He thought there was something else behind the thoughts, pushing them out into his mind. Something telling him something else.

The narrator came back to him for the first time in aeons. *You want to live, Papa,* it said. *You do not want to die here at the bottom of the pool.*

He pushed himself to his feet, stood in the shallow water. He

breathed in the warm air. His chest began to shake from the cold water. His skin was chilled to the touch.

His chest heaved. Oxygen was finding its home again in his lungs.

*You did not want to die*, said the narrator. *And that is OK.*

Hemingway replied: 'It was chickenshit and false.'

*No.*

'Yes.'

His breathing relaxed. He wiped water from his eyes. He looked out towards Havana. He looked to the mountains where the rebels were. He breathed some more.

He looked out to the horizon. He looked at the calmness of the skies.

The narrator fell silent. No more words in his head. Back to the agony.

He breathed again.


The rebels came closer, and there was murder in the air. Hemingway thought of Spain. He remembered Robles and Dos Passos. He blamed himself. His narrator did not appear to tell him otherwise.

He saw the changing of the political season. He saw the murderers in different clothes. He asked Miss Mary to go with him to Idaho. She agreed.

They flew to the new house in Ketchum. On the way there, he leaned over and took Miss Mary by the arm, and he said, 'I hope this plane goes down, Kitten, because then it will all be over.'

He watched boxing on television. He went out and hunted with their friends. Miss Mary went with him.

The rebels in Cuba won. Going home would be harder. The world turned on him.

It was cold in Idaho. He wanted to think of other things. He wanted to escape from his present.

His mind went back to earlier days. He thought about Paris, when it was just Hadley, Bumby and him, all together in a cold apartment on the rue Notre-Dame-des-Champs.

He thought of Hadley and Bumby in the snow in Austria, waiting for him. He squeezed tight his eyes to make the picture more vivid.

*They were never more beautiful*, he thought.

Miss Mary understood. He was more peaceful when half of his mind was elsewhere in Paris. She suggested they go there for more colour. 'You should write about this, Papa,' she said.

He and Miss Mary aimed for Paris, but they stopped first in Spain. They followed the festivities and the bullfighters around the country, part of the travelling, nomadic circus that went along behind the *toreros*. Papa wanted a new edition of *Death in the Afternoon*, and he resisted attempts to write anything else. He did not admit that his ability to write was clipped.

His mind was failing him. He turned sixty and he continued to drink hard. He berated Miss Mary over everything. She told him she would leave him but never did.

Spain exhausted them, three months of travel. They went to Paris with his new assistant Valerie. Hemingway eyed her, thought of her as family. Miss Mary rolled her eyes. She remembered the infatuation with Adriana. They stopped at the Ritz for lunch.

It was October in Paris when the weather began to turn and the heat of the summer shifted to the cold and damp brown of autumn, leaves falling from the trees and jackets swapped out for coats. The

ground was often wet, and the chill felt as if it were around the corner, waiting to enter the year.

Orson Welles sat by himself at a table in the corner of the restaurant of the Ritz. A plump capon was brought to his table, along with the wine, and he began to stab and tear at the food on the plate in front of him.

The food tasted good, brief moments when his problems and his pressures receded a little. He heard the word 'no' so many times when he was working that it felt, when he was eating, that he was getting a long series of yeses. He gulped at the wine and wiped at the corner of his mouth with the napkin.

He was fat, and he felt it. His hair felt lank and greasy, and he struggled to bring his stomach into his trousers, straining to close the button above the fly. He had already had them loosened twice by a seamstress, and he felt the shake of his jowls when he moved his head from one side to the other.

He was tired and he was frustrated. The money for *Don Quixote* had gone quickly, and he had come up to Paris to see what he could film and how. He needed more money and, as it had become evident from his dealing with the tax authorities, he needed that money quickly.

Hemingway went to the *maître d'*, a tall and thin man in a white jacket with a long nose, and he said nothing. He knew the man would know him, the most famous American writer of Paris, so he stopped as Miss Mary and Valerie came in behind him after shaking their umbrellas loose of the late autumn rain.

The *maître d'* looked back at the old man in front of him who was stooped a little and had thinning, white hair. Hemingway wore a brown jacket and dark trousers, with a white-spotted tie. He slumped

a little in the shoulders, as if life had taken as much from him as he had of it, and his beard was also white and clipped neatly.

'Sir?' The *maître d*'s eyes opened widely, and he looked down at the list in front of him on his small wooden lectern. 'I see you have a reservation.'

'I do.' Hemingway half-wished the man had spoken to him in French. He would have liked to reply in the same manner.

'It's an honour to have you here—'

'Thank you.'

'—Mr Welles.'

Hemingway bristled. 'It's Hemingway.'

The eyes of the *maître d'* flicked wide, then narrowed to their usual gimlet angle. He bowed his head. 'I apologise, Mr Hemingway. It is not often that we get such distinguished American guests at our hotel, and I made a mistake.'

Hemingway bristled some more. 'It's quite all right,' he said, anger in his chest.

The *maître d'* bowed again. 'Again, I am sorry, sir.' He looked down at his list once more. 'I see your name now. It is a table for three, yes?'

'Yes.'

'Please follow me.'

Hemingway, Miss Mary and Valerie were sat at a table, and they began to eat. Valerie looked over to a corner of the restaurant.

'Is that Orson Welles?' she asked Hemingway.

'It is, daughter,' he said.

'You know him, don't you?'

'On and off. For many years.'

'He reminds me of my uncle. He's so fat.'

Miss Mary looked at Valerie. 'Your uncle?'

'Why, yes. I'd love to meet him.' She looked at Hemingway. 'Would that be possible, Papa?'

Hemingway looked over at Welles. He signalled the *maître d'* to come back and said, 'Would you be so kind as to ask Mr Welles to join us? And if not, would you please take him a brandy from me to go with his coffee?'

The *maître d'* nodded once more. 'Yes, sir,' he said. His apologies still seemed to hang in the air.

Welles lumbered over a few moments later, the brandy in his hand. He seemed to be sweating. He smiled widely and boomed, 'Papa, what are you doing here?' He looked at Miss Mary and at Valerie. 'Tell me, Papa,' he said, without pausing, 'are these two young ladies your daughters?'

Hemingway stood and embraced Welles. He saw the folds in his face and the filled-out spaces of his skin. While he seemed to have lost weight, Welles had gained it. It was as if they were two people on opposite-travelling escalators, waving to each other as they passed by.

'It's good to see you, Orson,' Hemingway said. 'It's been too long. When was it? Venice?'

'I think so.'

'And yet we have not forgotten each other?'

'We have not.'

The *maître d'* brought one more chair and Miss Mary moved over, so that Welles could sit next to her husband. Some white screens were placed around them for privacy.

'What are you doing here, Mr Welles?' Miss Mary asked.

Welles placed his hand upon her arm briefly. 'Well, my dear, I'm here to try to raise money for some films that I'm trying to make. It's much harder now than it ever has been before. I'm sure you can

imagine. And to be honest, I thought it was so much of a wasted trip that I felt I had no choice but to call this a disappointment.' He stopped and sipped at his brandy. 'But now I have had the good fortune to run into your husband, it has become something of a success.'

'And why is it only "something" of a success, Mr Welles?'

'Orson, my dear. Call me "Orson". It's a success, because I came here hoping against hope that you would arrive! The downside is that you have arrived with your husband, so I have no chance of stealing you away from him!' Welles playfully put his hand on Hemingway's arm. His audience – Hemingway, Miss Mary, Valerie – smiled. 'And you, dear Papa, what are you doing here?'

'We have been in Spain, following the bulls, and now we are here in Paris. We go back to New York in a day or two.'

'Then Cuba? Nasty business down there.'

'Indeed.'

Welles heard the conversation begin to enter the valley of a lull. 'Tell me, how were the bulls this year? And, more importantly, how were the men that fought them? I hear that you are also friends with Ordóñez?'

'I am. And he fought well. We have been following him and Dominguín, to see who would have the better of each other.'

'And?'

'They have both fought well.'

Welles nodded. He let his head nod slightly, as if he were dredging up some deep thought and cleaning it free of muck. 'I believe that Ordóñez is the better of the pair. The better artist, at least, if you count the bullfight as art – and I do.'

Hemingway nodded back. 'We have some agreement there,' he said. He paused. 'You know, this may be the first time that we have ever agreed on anything, Orson.'

Welles looked at the old man in front of him. He thought Hemingway seemed depleted, as if he had burned off too early some of his internal reserves. 'And how goes it, Papa?' he asked. 'Are you a grandfather yet?'

Hemingway nodded. 'Yes. Two. Both with Bumby – I mean Jack, my eldest.'

'More boys?'

'Granddaughters. Joan and Margot. I don't see them so much.'

Welles pulled out a cigar and lit it. The rich smell of the burning tobacco began to curl into the room. 'I have another daughter now,' he said, 'but still no sons.'

Miss Mary smiled. There was a shard of misery in her voice. She thought of the 'Bridget' who had never arrived. 'How nice,' she said.

Welles continued talking. He reached into his jacket and pulled out a small photograph of his new daughter. He showed it first to Miss Mary, then to Hemingway.

Hemingway squinted at the picture. 'She is the most beautiful child,' he said.

'Thank you.' Welles showed the picture to Valerie, too, then put it away. 'She is, indeed, the light of my life,' he said.

Hemingway coughed. 'Are you still making films, Orson?'

'When I can, my dear. When I can. It seems to get harder each year.'

'Yet everyone loves you.'

Welles smiled. He winked at Miss Mary and Valerie. 'The problem, dear Papa, is that the people who say they love you – well, it's the sort of relationship where they adore you but never want to get into bed with you!'

Hemingway, Miss Mary and Valerie laughed. Some red rose in the cheeks of the ladies. 'Mr Welles,' said Miss Mary.

'Orson, please. And I do apologise – it seems that I may have gone too far with that last comment?'

Miss Mary touched his arm. 'Not at all, Orson. Why, I was also a war correspondent like my husband. There's not much about men that shocks me.'

Welles smiled. 'Very well, Mrs Hemingway.'

'Call me "Mary".'

'Very well, Mary.' Welles nodded his head at Miss Mary. He looked at the younger woman. 'And who might you be, my dear?'

Miss Mary spoke for her. 'This is Valerie. She's working as an assistant to Papa.'

Welles looked at Valerie. 'And how are you finding it? Good?'

Valerie blushed. She haltered and stammered over her words. 'It's interesting. Educational.'

Welles laughed, and it filled the room like oil being poured into a basin. '*Educational*,' he said. 'My dear, I hear an Irish accent in there. Am I right in thinking you're from Dublin?'

'I am.'

'A fine city. I was there when I was a boy, just before my first trip to Spain. I persuaded the Abbey Theatre that I was a well-known actor of New York.' He whispered the next part, then spoke normally. '*I was seventeen.* And they put me on the stage where I was possibly the worst actor that the Emerald Isle had ever seen.'

Welles stopped, expecting laughter. There was a stiff chuckle from Valerie and Miss Mary. 'I loved you in *The Third Man*,' Valerie said, eventually.

'That music follows me everywhere,' he said, ruefully. 'Or it did. Not so much now, but I feel that it will be the part I'm best remembered for, if anyone remembers me at all. But that is not a bad thing – it's probably the best part written for an actor in this

century. And I wrote some of it for myself. Not most, just a little. But your Graham Greene is a tremendous author and Carol Reed a tremendous director. I am lucky to have had it and that it did not end up with Bob Mitchum or Jimmy Mason.'

'I think they would have been good, too, in the part.'

'I agree. Anyone would have. But it's a wonderful part, and I'm glad that it was mine.' Welles laughed again.

Miss Mary stood up. She motioned to Valerie. 'If you would excuse us, Orson, Valerie and I have some business to take care of. May I leave you here with Papa?'

'Of course.' Welles and Hemingway rose to acknowledge the leaving of Miss Mary and Valerie, then sat once more.

Welles saw that Hemingway looked drawn. He noted the sag in his shoulders, and he put his hand on one of them, by Hemingway's neck, and he felt the sharp bone beneath the line of the jacket.

'Are you well, Papa?'

'I am, Orson.'

'Very well, Papa.'

Hemingway ordered another round of drinks. They sat in silence while they waited for them to come. When they came, Hemingway picked his up with a trembling hand and sipped at it. 'These bones are getting old,' he said, and there was sadness in his voice.

Welles nodded. No performance, just an acknowledgement. 'I know.'

'You were so vibrant when I first met you. You seemed like you were going to have everything. I'm sorry if I speak out of turn here. I've been thinking a lot about the past, you see. Everything was so much brighter back then. When my boys were young, I thought that they could be anything – that they would be *everything*. But life hasn't worked out that way, I guess.'

'No, Papa, it hasn't.'

'You were going to have everything.'

'And I didn't. And you did have everything.'

'And I lost it. That film you made, the one about the newspaperman?'

'*Citizen Kane*?'

'Yes. Did you ever take heat for that?'

'Some. Everyone thought it was based on Hearst, and I suppose you could have seen it that way if you squinted. But it wasn't. Not strictly. There were many people who sat for that. But Hearst's people around him thought it was about him, and they tried to destroy me in order to curry his favour.'

'Do you regret it?'

'No. I had the ignorance then that I'd never have again. That's how we came up with so many new things. No one ever told us that we couldn't. And I liked Kane as a character. I saw him as tragic, which no one else seemed to. Apart from the Soviets – they still don't play that picture in Russia. I was too gentle to a capitalist, they say. I made him too human.'

'Was that the story?'

'I think so. Yes, looking back, that was always the story.' Welles reached up and took hold of Hemingway's shoulder again, and he looked him in the eye. Hemingway's body trembled. 'It was about a man of real gifts and charm and humanity who destroyed himself and everything near him.'

'Do you know what's left, Orson?'

Welles shook his head. 'No.'

'The first thing that a man must do is endure. And the second is that a man must die.'

Afterwards, Hemingway and Welles walked out of the Ritz and onto the streets of Paris. Hemingway going in one direction, Welles another. They went out of the front doors, arm in arm, and stood for a few moments in the chilling air, each marking wordlessly how the season was changing and how the air seemed to be carrying the hint of mist within it.

Hemingway reached into his jacket pocket and took out a small hard object that was a couple of inches long and wrapped in tissue paper. He handed it to Welles, who felt its heaviness.

'A harmonica?'

'No, Orson, a knife.'

'A knife?'

Welles unwrapped the knife, crunching the tissue paper in his hand into a ball. The knife was a small one carried usually by the Swiss Army. There was a white cross embossed onto its red handle. Welles hooked a fingernail into the crevice on the side of the blade and pulled it out about half an inch. He looked back at Hemingway.

'I'm starting a club,' Hemingway said. 'You are a capital fellow, Orson, and should be in it. Everyone will have the same knife. Let me give you this one. It's mine, but I will be buying more.'

'Thank you, Papa.'

A car went past, through the centre of the Place Vendôme, and the pair followed it with their eyes. 'The world is changing, Orson,' Hemingway said, and there was a melancholy timbre to his voice. 'Let's meet again here in a few days,' he said.

'Yes, let's do that.'

The rain was beginning to fall a little heavier. They unlinked arms, and Welles went in his direction, and Hemingway in his. Although they had planned to meet again, they had not fixed a date. Both

knew that such things were superfluous. There was a singular truth that was missing from their conversation, hidden like the depths of an iceberg – these two men would never again meet face to face.

# 12

# THE FINAL DAYS OF ERNEST HEMINGWAY (1960 TO 1961)

It was 1960, and Ernest Hemingway was living in Ketchum, Idaho, where he still liked to rise early each morning when the air was cool, go to his desk and try to write. He wanted to find, if he could, just a single, true word. But he found, now aged sixty-one, that his narrator no longer came to him.

He tended to leave his bed at seven, pad lightly past the bedroom in which Miss Mary slept and stand at his desk in the room that overlooked the Big Wood River that ran past his house and along the border of his land. He liked to see the mallards feeding on the watercress at the bottom of the slope, and he would look then to the cold emptiness and try to think of words. But he found that the words no longer came to him and those that did came without the clarity they had once had.

Eventually, he would submit quietly to fate around lunchtime and go for a long walk along the roads by his house, waving to school-children as they finished their day. And each time, as he trudged along the road, lighter in the step from all that lost weight, he would reassure himself that he would write well again one day. It was

important to keep trying, and he would tell himself each afternoon that he had not only tried that day but that he had tried the day before, too, and that he would try again the day after.

When the cold winds rolled over the Idaho hills around the house, he thought of the Finca Vigía, on the outskirts of Havana. His home, now in the middle of a war. He thought of the heat in the air and the smells of verbena and bougainvillea, and how they mixed with those of the jacaranda and the frangipani, and there was a clawing thought in his chest that he would never see it or Cuba or Spain again. And those cold Idaho winds would roll across the hills and the trees and into the empty space of his mind, and then roll out once more, and still the words were no longer there.

There were days when he knew that he would never write again. And it was on those days when he knew that what he was writing was poor – a Paris memoir that was going nowhere, a book about sex that he felt he could never publish. He felt the shifts as the world rolled around him into new ages, and he felt cycled between unfinished books.

And he knew, too, that he had burned out whatever talent he had once had and all that was left were his own ghosts. And when he knew he could not write and that he had dwelled long upon it, he felt hopeless and impotent.

He was growing old, and he hated it – hated the pills and potions that they gave him for his liver and his kidneys, and the way he shook sometimes when he felt his anxiety rise. He hated the eyesight that blurred and was leaking colours, and he hated how the doctors would force him through Miss Mary to watch what he ate and drank. He took his weight throughout the day, marvelling at each half pound lost or feeling the gloom of it gained after eating, and he had Dr Saviers come each lunchtime to take his blood pressure.

Each evening, he and Miss Mary would drive ten minutes into the

centre of the small town where they would eat dinner at the Christiania. It was there that she kept her eyes on him while he scanned the room for 'the shadow people' that he knew were following them. If they managed to sit through the whole meal without him making them bolt for the door, then he would drive them back afterwards to the house, where they would sit and drink coffee and think about what adventures they might take again one day.

One night, he and Miss Mary were in the Christiania, and he looked out to the bank on the other side of the street where they had their accounts. It was dark outside, the winter's snow beginning to fall, and it was cold, but there were lights on in the building and there were shadows moving around inside.

Hemingway began to shake. He put down his knife and his fork, and he jabbed Miss Mary in the side with his elbow, and he leaned over by a degree or two, and he whispered to her without taking his eyes from the building.

'Do you see that?' he asked.

'See what?'

'The lights over there.' He gripped his knife and drew it towards him. 'The lights. That's them, right now, going through our accounts. They're auditing us.'

Miss Mary sighed. Her shoulders slumped. She had heard these fears before. 'Papa,' she said, simply.

'Miss Mary, they're shadow people. They're looking to get us for something. That's why they're looking at our accounts now. They're trying to find something to pin upon me. They're out to get me. Can't you see?'

'Do you want to go, Papa?'

He turned and looked at her. 'That's what *you* want,' he said. '*You*

want them to get me. No, I'm going to sit here and see what they do.' He gripped the knife again. 'And I'll fight them if they come for us now. I won't let them take you.'

'Papa, they're probably just the cleaners working at night.'

'Why now, Miss Mary? Why would they be working *now*?'

'It's October, and the winter is drawing in. They always work at this time; they just need the lights on now.'

'I don't like it, Miss Mary. I don't like it.'

'I know, Papa. I know.'

'They're trying to get me, you see. They want me. It's to do with tax. State tax, federal tax. They want me for something like that. It's the girl, too. Valerie. They want me because of her visa. I know I shouldn't have employed her back home. That's what they're going to get me for. They're going to use her to get to me, but I did nothing wrong with her apart from pay her some cash for her studies in New York. I was just doing that, and that's what they're going to get me for.'

Miss Mary sighed. She pushed away her coffee. She put her hand on her husband's arm. She squeezed his wrist. 'Let's go, Papa,' she said. 'Let's go back to the house.'

'What if it's bugged? I know it's bugged. The car, too. They can hear everything we say.'

'Then we shall talk of beautiful things. No one can terrorise us for talking of beautiful things.'

Hemingway looked at Miss Mary. His eyes were wet, and his body trembled. 'I'm sorry, Miss Mary,' he said, 'that you're here with me in this. I shall try to protect you. I'll write to everyone who matters, and I'll tell them that you had nothing to do with any of it, that you were operating on the "false" numbers I gave you. Hopefully, they'll go light on you. And if they don't, then they *are* sons of bitches.'

Miss Mary stood. She took her husband's arm and helped him

stand. She saw how thin he was, down to 164 pounds, and she saw how his jaw shook and of how much he looked like an old man. Not as old as he really was but much older, as if he were ageing beyond numbers. 'Come on, Papa,' she said, leading him towards the door. He took tiny steps like a schoolchild.

'We have to pay, Miss Mary,' Hemingway said. 'It's one more thing that they'll get me for.'

Miss Mary signalled the restaurateur, and she mouthed the word 'tomorrow'. The restaurateur nodded back; he had seen this before. 'It's OK, Papa,' she said. 'They know us. We can settle this tomorrow. Let's go.'

'Be careful outside, Miss Mary. You walk behind me, and you tell me if you can see them.' He flashed the knife. 'That way, I have a chance of fighting them.'

'No one is going to fight anyone, Papa.'

'I will, Miss Mary, if they come for you.'

'OK, Papa.'

'I love you, Miss Mary.'

'I love you, too.'

That night, after he had gone to sleep in his room, Miss Mary went to the kitchen and dialled Dr Saviers. She felt her chest shake. She tried to push back her tears, but they began to run down her face.

'Mrs Hemingway,' Dr Saviers said. 'It's late. Is everything OK?'

'No,' Miss Mary said. 'No, it's not. Can you come tomorrow?'

'Is it Papa?'

'Yes.'

Dr Saviers voice dropped. 'OK. I'll come tomorrow.'

'They'll think it,' said Hemingway, the next morning in his living

room. Miss Mary and Dr Saviers were watching him from the opposite side. They sat together on a long chair. 'They'll think it,' Hemingway said, again.

'Think what, Papa?' Dr Saviers asked.

'They'll think I'm losing my marbles. That's how they get you. They'll write me off as a crazy. They'll say, "Well, he's gone mad with the guilt." But I'm not guilty. I've done nothing.'

'I know, Papa.' Dr Saviers stood up. 'There are other things we can do,' he said, walking over. He crouched down in front of Hemingway. 'You keep records, yes? Of everything.'

'Yes.'

'OK. What was your blood pressure yesterday?'

'It was 250 over 125.'

'That's high, isn't it?' Dr Saviers patted Hemingway's knee. 'Why don't we say it's to do with that? No one will know. We shall keep it to ourselves.'

Hemingway looked at Dr Saviers. His eyes were wide. 'Please help me,' he said.

Miss Mary knelt in front of her husband. She put her hands on his leg. 'He will, Papa.'

Hemingway looked at Dr Saviers. 'She wants me away, so she can take my money,' he said.

Miss Mary closed her eyes. There were no longer any tears. 'I don't, Papa,' she said.

Hemingway shook his head. 'You can't trust them, Doctor,' he said. 'You can't trust anyone. All of them are murderers. They just come in different clothes. Can't trust any of them.'

Dr Saviers nodded. 'I'm just a local doctor, Papa. This isn't my area. But I want you to go to the Menninger Clinic in Kansas. They'll take care of you.'

'That's a mental hospital?'

'It is.'

'I can't let them think I'm nuts. Can't let that happen. That's how they get you.'

'What about Mayo? That hospital is for body and mind. We'll say it's for your blood pressure. The government are not going to know about it.'

'I can't let them think I'm crazy.'

Dr Saviers nodded as if the matter was decided. 'I'll make the call,' he said.

The plane left Idaho early and rose up into the cold air. It was a small plane that had been rented privately and there were four people on board: Ernest Hemingway, Mary Welsh Hemingway, Dr Saviers and the pilot. It turned east and flew first over Wyoming, then across Nebraska and Iowa, before coming to land at an airport seven miles outside of Rochester, Minnesota, where the Mayo Clinic was located.

Dr Saviers took Hemingway to St Mary's Hospital, which was on the campus's north-west corner. He had called ahead and told the administration that America's most famous writer was on his way, was suffering from paranoia and delusional thinking and had fears that the world would discover he was mentally ill. The administration agreed to house him at St Mary's, where the patients with rheumatism and arthritis were treated.

Hemingway was to be given a private room. The nun in attendance asked him basic questions when he arrived.

'Your name is Ernest Miller Hemingway,' she said. 'When were you born?'

Hemingway shook his head. He could not remember.

Dr Saviers leaned in. 'He was born on 21 July 1899,' he said. 'The patient is sixty-one years old.'

The nun turned to Hemingway. 'What's your address?'

Hemingway shook his head. 'I don't know,' he mumbled.

'Next of kin?'

Hemingway shook his head. 'I think she wants me here,' he said.

The nun noted this down. 'How much do you weigh, Mr Hemingway?'

Hemingway shook his head.

Dr Saviers leaned in again. 'He was 164 pounds, as of yesterday morning.'

Hemingway shook. 'Please help me,' he said.

The nun nodded. 'Any history of mental illness within the family?'

Hemingway looked at her. 'My father came here fifty-one years ago,' he said. 'He was a doctor. He toured here.'

The nun looked at Dr Saviers. 'Any history of mental illness?'

Hemingway coughed. 'He killed himself, about my age. I come from men who kill themselves. I killed all those animals so I could hold off from killing myself.'

'That is not going to happen, Papa,' Dr Saviers said. 'The people here are going to help you.'

The nun looked at Hemingway. 'And your mother?'

Hemingway snarled. His shoulders tensed. 'That old bitch,' he spat out. 'She drove my father to kill himself.'

The nun nodded and put down the paper on which she had been writing notes. 'I think we should get you settled in first, Papa,' she said. 'We have a private room for you, and we can finish the questions later. Right now, we'll put you down under your doctor's name – Dr Saviers.'

Two doctors saw Hemingway when he had arrived and settled in. They saw the hunched-over and frail-looking old man with the thin white hair and the jagged, angular frame who sat like a scared, lonely child on the bed.

It was the beginning of December in Minnesota, but the hospital was stuffy and warm from the large brass radiators that hissed when condensation fell from the inside of the high glass windows. Outside, in the distance, there was a frozen lake that seemed perfectly circular. In the summer and the autumn, the doctors would often hear the call of birds as they went into the air. In winter, it was the scrape of skates along its ice.

The doctors examined Hemingway. His muscles were toned beneath skin that seemed too thin, as fragile as tissue paper.

'How are you doing, Papa?' Dr Rome asked. 'How do you feel today?'

Hemingway did not answer. He looked out of the window and over to the pond, towards something that may have been in the distance. His mouth moved, but he made no sound. His lips tried to catch and hold onto words.

Dr Butt sat next to the patient. He rolled up the sleeve of Hemingway's gown. He pressed down on the sinewy joints and held his finger against Hemingway's pulse. He took out a stethoscope and a sphygmomanometer.

'Your blood pressure is down, Papa,' Dr Butt said, eventually. 'It's 160 over ninety-eight. That's moving in the right direction.'

Hemingway stared outside.

Dr Butt carried on. 'We've run some tests,' he said. 'We can see that you have a mild case of diabetes, and your liver is enlarged. We also think you have haemochromatosis, where your body cannot

absorb all the iron in your blood. It's often hereditary, and we understood that your father had it. The problem is that we cannot run the tests for it. They're too invasive for you.'

Hemingway turned. His eyes were vacant. He was afraid, could not understand why he was still alive.

Dr Butt said, 'Your physician in Idaho says that you have been on Serpasil and Ritalin.'

Hemingway said nothing.

The doctor looked at his notes. 'The Serpasil is a problem,' he said. 'It can make you depressed. I think that may be what we have here. We'd like to move you to Librium, and we also have another treatment that we think may benefit you.'

Hemingway looked to the floor. He hooked his fingers into the bottom of his gown and tugged at its hem. 'Please help me,' he said.

'We can,' Dr Rome said. 'We're going to give you what is known as ECT – electroconvulsive therapy.' He sat down on the bed, and he placed his index fingers on Hemingway's temples. 'We're going to use something that will send a current between this finger and that finger, right through your head. It should make you better. It's like a reset.'

Hemingway nodded. 'My sons,' he rasped.

Dr Butt looked at him. 'Your sons?'

'Patrick and Gregory. They did that to them, too.' His mind flashed back to Patrick in 1947, and the concussion and the weeks that followed, how the doctors had blasted through his brain and of how the boy had been fine afterwards. He thought of Gig in 1957 and of how that had not helped. 'My boys,' he said.

The doctors nodded.

The doctors took Hemingway in the next few days, and they began

to run electric shocks through his brain, making him convulse on gurneys in their clinic. Hemingway lay there in a white gown, his bowels and bladder empty, and he bit down on a piece of rubber as the doctors put the electrodes on his temples and shocked him. His vision whitened and his body tensed, and then he shook for some seconds, before going limp. Afterwards, they would wheel him back to his private room, where he would sleep and rest, before they came back a day or so later and did it again. He began to lose count of the shocks as the weeks went by, and he became used to the white blasts that shook his ailing brain. And he felt at times that they took with them the poison of his mind, and in the other times they seemed to take everything else.

He lay in his cot one afternoon when the noise of the ward had fallen a little. The nurses had shooed the patients to their beds so that they might sleep, and he lay in the warm, muggy air in his clean, white sheets, and he began to think once more about Paris. He thought that he may take Miss Mary there again, back to the Ritz or the six-day bicycle races near the Eiffel Tower.

And then he realised that he did not remember the name of the track, although he had been there many times in the 1920s with Hadley and for the last races with Miss Mary a few years before. And then he realised that he could not recall the name of the man there who took his bets or the one who made sure his drinks never ran dry.

He took his mind back to other places and realised that vast swathes of them were lost in his recollection. Names, faces, facts had disappeared, their absence filled with grey smoke and vapours. He jumped his thoughts to the Hotel Florida in Madrid, to 1937 with her, the third wife whose name he refused to speak, and he tried to remember the funny little Frenchman who had given out the grapefruits during a bombing raid or the commie reporter from

England who had escaped from a Berlin cabaret. Their names were also lost in grey smoke.

Hemingway began to cry and shake, and the nuns came in, and they sat and held his hand. He explained to them what had happened, that all he had known had gone away, and he wept some more, and they called one of the doctors to come over to him.

'Papa,' said Dr Butt when he arrived, 'it is distressing but not uncommon. Those memories of yours will come back. You are already much better.'

The newspapers knew by January that Hemingway was at the Mayo Clinic, and they came to its grounds to seek him out. America's – and, arguably, the world's – most famous writer, the manliest of men, was in hospital. The scuttlebutt was that he was taken with madness.

The nuns saw the newspapermen hunched in the cold, looking in windows to see if the old and broken man was there, and they despaired. They put out a statement and said that Hemingway was there only for the treatment of his high blood pressure.

They released him in January, and they said he was cured, and so Miss Mary came to Minnesota where she collected him, and they flew back to Idaho.

She watched him on the plane back. His shoulders trembled. She still saw the fear in his eyes. She saw the worry in his face. She thought he was scared that it might happen again.

'Papa?' she asked, over the din of the engine. He ignored her. 'Papa?' she called again. He looked at her this time. 'We're going home.'

He smiled, and it was the grin of someone near derangement. He nodded. 'I know, Miss Mary,' he said. 'I know.'

The weeks ticked by. The winter peaked, then began to trough. Idaho began to thaw, and the first sounds of birds began to appear. But Hemingway's mind still had the empty places, as if a blanket had been thrown over his memories. He pulled and tugged at the edge of that blanket to see if he could prompt an echo of what might have been beneath, but it remained firmly tamped down.

Each morning, he went to his desk and stood and tried to write, but there was nothing there. The electricity had shaken those things loose from his mind. *They will come back to you*, the doctors told him, so he waited, but they never came.

The words seemed to be gone, and his mind went to other places. He walked around their Ketchum home, and he told Miss Mary that it was the FBI and that they were after him and how he wished that they would leave him alone.

'You will be fine', he told her, 'because they will know that you have worked with them to get me. And that is fine, too, because I see clearly now, and I know it is not hopeless because I know what it is that they – and *you* – are doing to me.'

The new Kennedy administration invited him to the inauguration in February 1961. Miss Mary, on his behalf, turned down the invite on the grounds of his health, citing his high blood pressure and the injuries from the African plane crashes.

The new President's people, in reply, asked for a few lines of tribute to be given to Kennedy as he entered the White House.

Hemingway went to his desk. He took out his typewriter, as he had in the olden days, and he began to write. He hacked at each key and each time when he finished, he found the work unsatisfactory or just bad, and so he took the paper and screwed it up in his hand and dropped it desultorily into the bin. And then he would start again.

Dr Saviers came one day to take his blood pressure. He found Hemingway standing in the room in which he wrote. There were tears on the blank paper.

'It is not there any more, George,' he said. 'It is not there.'

Eventually, he wrote, with the harsh winds blowing across his mind: *It is a good thing to have a brave man as our President in times as tough as these are for our country and the world.*

In April 1961, around two weeks before he took his own life, Ernest Hemingway watched from his home in Ketchum, Idaho, as a US-backed force of Cuban rebels, aided by the CIA, failed to oust Fidel Castro.

The men landed upon the beaches that lay to the south of Havana, then tried to make their way to the capital, but they were repelled within days, the US defeated heavily in front of billions. The JFK administration was forced to pay millions in reparations and hand over tonnes of humanitarian aid. The oily man in the greasy, green uniform with the beard and the cigars laughed in front of the planet at the world's strongest superpower.

In Idaho, Hemingway and Miss Mary watched the action unfold on the small television in their home. Hemingway shook, his mind going to their home on Cuban shores – the place he had lived in for twenty years, along with it his books and their animals, their staff who would now come under suspicion.

He was reading a newspaper, and tears fell upon it, and the ink began to run and smear his fingertips as he throttled through its pages.

'It's gone,' he said, with a deep, immeasurable sadness of a dream finally being snuffed away. His voice shook, and he said to Miss Mary, 'All of it – it's gone.'

Miss Mary came down into the living room the next day and saw Hemingway sat on the sofa, his shotgun in his hand. He was wearing the deep-red robe she had bought for him in Italy, and he was positioned to see her as she walked in. His shoulders were slumped, and he wore nothing beneath the robe.

'Papa,' she said. 'You never bring your guns into the house. You always keep them downstairs. You are so safe with them.'

Hemingway nodded, slightly. The gun was open and resting on his knee. Miss Mary could see that the barrel was empty. She saw some shells within reach of Papa, and she knew that he intended to reach out when he had gathered his bravery, take them, put them into the gun, then shoot himself.

'Papa,' she said, again. 'What are you doing?'

'Here,' he said, gruffly. 'It's all in here.' He reached into the pocket of his robe and pulled out a note, then handed it to her. 'No point staying around, is there?'

Miss Mary looked at the note. There were words, but they added up to no logic. She saw sentences that began with a word or two but then fell off. Hemingway had written the letter in one direction, then another, and then a third, so that it was impossible to know in what order all of it had come to him. That was if there had been any order at all. 'Papa,' she said.

Hemingway put the gun to one side and stood up. He came to her and took the note, put it back in his pocket. 'I really shouldn't hang around any more,' he said, sitting back down and putting the gun across his knee.

'Hang around for what, Papa?'

'Isn't it obvious, Miss Mary?'

'No.'

He looked away, as if to change subject. 'I hate this time of year,'

he said. 'It's a middling, in-between time. No heat, no cold – just something freezing or thawing. At least in September, the leaves begin to fall. But not in April. Not here.'

Miss Mary flinched as Hemingway put his hand on the sofa, his fingers five inches or so away from the loose shells. 'Papa, this is not bravery,' she said. 'Not to go like this.'

'I have endured, Miss Mary, and now I must die.'

Tears sprang into her eyes, and Miss Mary saw her husband swim in her vision. He was blurry for a moment until she blinked, and then he was back. *So old, so thin*, she thought. 'You still have things to do,' she said, her voice cracking.

Hemingway shook his head.

Miss Mary begged. 'Yes, yes. And your boys. They need you. John and Patrick and Greg. They need their father.'

Hemingway put his chin upon his chest. Some tears fell onto the thin skin there, and he shook his head. 'I can't any more,' he said. 'Can't that be *enough*?'

Miss Mary wept. She pushed her tears away from her cheeks, and she breathed in, hard. She steadied her voice. 'Papa,' she said. 'I am afraid. I want to take the gun, but I am afraid that I might get shot.'

Hemingway looked at her, tears in his eyes. He shook his head. 'But I love you, Miss Mary,' he said. 'No danger here.'

'I know, Papa. But accidents do happen.'

They sat like this for some time. Eventually, Dr Saviers came and knocked on the door, and he saw the gun on Hemingway's lap and the stiff back of Miss Mary, and he knew what was happening.

Dr Saviers came in, and he looked at Hemingway in the eye, and he took the gun from him, and he said, 'Papa, it's time to go back to the clinic. We have to treat you again. Roll up your sleeve.'

Hemingway nodded, in defeat. 'A man is broken,' he said, and he

rolled up his sleeve. In seconds, Dr Saviers had slipped the sodium amytal into his veins, and the old, broken man was asleep on the sofa.

The weather was bad for some days, and they could not fly. Dr Saviers moved Hemingway to a local hospital, where he kept him sedated. When the weather had improved by the end of the month, they took him back to his house so that he could pick up some belongings.

Hemingway was quiet on the journey, and he looked out at the hills of Idaho. He saw some children skipping by, and he waved to them out of habit, a smile upon his face. Then he sat back in the car and knew what he was going to do next.

When they got to the house, he waited until they were ready to go, and then he announced that he needed the bathroom. 'There's nowhere to piss on that plane,' he said in a light growl, then headed without saying anything else into his home.

Inside, he made a dash for the stairs, and he managed to get down into the basement where the guns were kept. He got one into his hands and was feeding a shell into it when two strong men, Dr Saviers and an orderly from the hospital, wrenched the gun from him and pushed him to the floor.

They took him outside and put him back into the car, then drove quickly to the airport where they bundled him onto a plane. As it took off, Hemingway smiled once more, then leaned over and tried to unlock the door.

'Papa!' Dr Saviers yelled, pulling him back into his seat.

Hemingway lied. 'I just wanted to check it,' he said.

The plane landed to refuel in Rapid City an hour later. Hemingway walked off, the orderly behind him, and he went to the cars

parked outside. Most of them were unlocked, and he began to open the doors and search them.

The orderly came up behind him. 'Is it the FBI, Papa?'

'Yes, that's it. I'm looking for the FBI.' Hemingway laughed to himself. *IT'S NOT THE FBI*, he thought. *I'M LOOKING FOR A GUN. I'LL END THIS NOW.*

'We're going now.'

'OK.' Hemingway turned and walked towards their plane. Out on the tarmac, there was another vehicle with its engine running. Hemingway saw its propellor turn with a *thrum* that beckoned him.

*THIS IS IT*, he thought, and he began to stride over. *THIS IS IT.* He walked away from Dr Saviers, and the orderly, and his life with Miss Mary, and he headed towards the *thrum* that he felt matched the long, distant fizz inside his own head, and he knew he was heading home. He began to feel the reverberations of the movement of the wings, and he felt a tingle in his fingertips as he drew near.

The noise stopped, a metallic and mechanical whine rising as the *thrum* fell away. Hemingway opened his eyes, and he saw the plane's propellor slowing. He felt a strong hand on his arm.

'It's time to go, Papa,' a shaking voice said in his ear. 'It's time to go.'

That night, Hemingway and Dr Saviers came to the Mayo Clinic where, this time, he checked in under his own name. Then, once the doctors and the nuns had seen him once more, they took him to the ward where such troubled patients stayed, and they locked him in a room by himself.

Once inside, sedated, Hemingway began to sleep once more.

On the door outside, somebody wrote on the sign: *Former writer, do not disturb.*

The doctors came in the next days, and they shocked his brain once more with the white blasts. *There is nothing else we can do*, they would tell him, and then they would shock him again. Four times in five days, much more than in the first visit.

Hemingway acquiesced. He liked the bliss of not knowing, of not remembering. He wished that they could continue blasting him and that he could carry on not knowing and not remembering.

He liked to think that this was how it should always have been.

A few weeks later, Hemingway was with Dr Rome. The two of them sat in his office, and Dr Rome asked Hemingway how he was feeling.

'I'm good,' he said. *I KNOW WHAT IS GOING ON NOW*, he thought. *IT'S MISS MARY, AND SHE'S PUT ME HERE SO THAT SHE CAN TAKE ALL MY MONEY*. Hemingway smiled.

'Are you OK, Papa?'

'I am.'

'Do you still want to die?'

*YES*. 'No, not here. I want to go home.'

'You want to go home and die?'

*YES, I DO*. 'No, I don't. I just want to go home.'

'Well, we don't want you to die, Papa.'

Hemingway nodded. He smiled. He tried to make it sound like a joke. 'Well, I can promise you that I won't kill myself here,' he said.

The doctors called Miss Mary at the end of June, and they told her that her husband was well enough to be discharged. She hurried over to Dr Rome's office and when she got there to argue that it was too soon, her husband was sitting waiting for her. He was dressed in his street clothes, a hat on his knee.

Miss Mary stopped. She took a breath and put a hand to her chest. She saw the old and broken man. She could not understand why the doctors could not see the same thing.

'Papa?' she asked.

Hemingway nodded. Hemingway smiled. He stood up, a smile like a leer on his face. 'I'm well now, Miss Mary,' he said. 'I want to go home.'

It was the first of July, and Hemingway had been home for two days, and so he and Miss Mary went that night into Ketchum to eat dinner at the Christiania.

They sat with friends, and the wine and the food came, and Hemingway joked a little, although it was forced, as if he were pretending to her and to them that he was the same again and that it had all been a silly little misadventure.

There were two men at the end of the bar. They were dressed in sober, boring suits, and one of them had hair that was slicked down and the other was balding. They were each drinking a beer, and they did not move their eyes towards the Hemingways' table. They were not talking, sitting beside each other in silence.

Hemingway saw them. He stiffened, and he called over the restaurant owner.

'Who are those two men?' he asked, his voice faltering.

Miss Mary saw what was happening. She closed her eyes. She felt the falling sense of dread in her chest.

'Which two men, Papa?' the owner said.

'There,' Hemingway said, with a small nod of his head, his eyes averted. 'Those two men at the bar.'

The owner of the restaurant turned in their direction. He looked at the bar. 'Oh, those two men? They're just salesmen, Papa. They

come through here once a month on business. We see them all the time.'

Hemingway looked at the men, but he knew that if asked to write about them in the morning that he would struggle to describe them. Their faces were too common, too much like those of middle-aged, forgettable men everywhere that anyone could have described them narrowly. *Those men*, he thought, *who would have bought my books and now they hunt me.* 'Thank you,' he said, quietly, and then he squeezed the restaurant owner's arm.

Miss Mary leaned over. 'Is everything in order, Papa?' she asked.

Hemingway nodded. 'It's the FBI, Miss Mary. They're back again.'

Later that night, after their guests had gone home and they were getting ready for their beds, Hemingway and Miss Mary hummed together an Italian tune that they had both once known. Now, only Miss Mary remembered its name, the white blasts of the Mayo Clinic having cleared it from her husband's recall.

Later, Miss Mary would remember her husband as being in a light mood as they said goodnight and before he shuffled down the hall to his own bedroom. She remembered the sound of him moving away, the light in the hallway still lit, and his final words to her: 'Goodnight, my kitten.'

On the last morning of his life, a former writer known as Ernest Hemingway woke at 7 a.m., got out of bed and put a deep-red robe on above his blue pyjamas. Careful not to wake his fourth wife, whom he called 'Miss Mary', he padded past her bedroom in the moccasins he used as slippers and went down to their kitchen, where he took from a shelf the key to the gun cabinet in the basement.

He then went cautiously down the stairs into the cold room and

took out the Scott shotgun he had bought some years before, put it beneath his arm and stiffly made his way back up to the kitchen, where he crossed over to the small vestibule that lay in front of the door to the outside.

There, he looked out once more onto the sharp hills of Idaho and, below all that, just out of sight beyond the trees, the Big Wood River that ran past his home. It was so early that the morning air still had some chill to it, and he imagined the emptiness of the outside and of the emptiness of the inside of his own head.

'It's time to go,' he said, to no one in particular. He wanted to say other words, but they were not there and had not been for some time. He slid one shell into the gun, then another, and he took a deep breath, and he felt the static fizz once more inside his head, and he realised for the last time that this, indeed, was his end.

He put the gun on the floor, then he leaned over and he pressed his forehead onto the cold metal of the barrel. He felt the edge of it push against his skin, stopping against the bone of his skull.

'It is time to go,' he said, slowly, enunciating the last of the words. Then, without saying anything else, he pushed his toe down on the gun's trigger.

After the police had come and gone, and the body of her husband had been taken away, Miss Mary took the Scott shotgun with her into the centre of Ketchum, and she handed it to a local welder. He, without saying anything, took the gun and dismantled it within his shop, breaking apart the stock and cutting the metal pieces with a torch. Later, he took the pieces out with him to a field within the Idaho countryside and buried them in a handful of secret places.

Two days later, there was a *torero* on the other side of the world who

was sitting on a patio in Biarritz, in the south of France. The *torero* was resting for a few days before Pamplona. He was eating breakfast at his hotel, along with his *cuadrilla*, and he liked to sit apart some mornings so that he would not be disturbed as he watched the coral waters lap at the beach's amber sands. That was what he was doing that morning when he felt the air shift, and he looked up to see a writer he knew looking at him. There were tears in the writer's eyes.

The *torero* knew it was serious. 'What is it?' he asked.

'It's Papa. He's dead.'

'Are you sure? He's been dead many times.'

'Yes.'

'How?'

'The wires say that he died accidentally, while cleaning his gun.'

'But he was always so careful with his guns. That is not what happened, is it?'

'Mary says so, but it's not true.'

The *torero* nodded. He looked over the water and to Spain. 'He's gone,' he said, after a few moments. 'I guess it really is all over.'

ACT THREE

# ONE BULL
# AT SUNDOWN
# (1961 TO 1985)

# 13

# SACRED BEASTS (1961, 1972)

*'Hemingway? That left hook of his was overrated.'*
– JAKE HANNAFORD, *THE OTHER SIDE OF THE WIND*

There was a loud bang as a gun was fired.

The shot startled the Pamplona crowd and the bulls that were about to chase them, and then the race was on through the streets all the way to the bullring. It was the day after the death of Ernest Hemingway.

High above the sea of people dressed in white flowing through the city, in the Gran Hotel La Perla, was Orson Welles. He was too big to run, almost too big to do anything, and so he filmed the crowd below as the men, their necks wrapped in red scarves, sprinted down Plaza del Castillo and beyond, passing by him. The bulls came after them and parts of the crowd moved to the side, splintering away from the phalanx of running people. Welles was bored with what he saw, but he kept the camera rolling so he could capture this version of Spain for the Italian TV company that was paying for this travelogue.

Eventually, the street began to turn back to normal as the crowd

went by, and although it was busy, it began to look once more like an average European street. Welles stepped away from the camera, lit a cigar and sat on one of the hotel room's comfier chairs.

Paola came into the room, then, and she put down in front of him the day's *International Herald Tribune*, along with a pot of coffee. She kissed him on the side of the forehead and then walked off towards their bedroom. He watched her move away, and he knew she was so much more than he had any right to expect.

She stopped at the door. 'You knew him, didn't you? Wasn't he your friend?'

'Who?'

'Hemingway.' She saw the look of confusion on his face. 'Look at the papers. He died yesterday.'

Welles looked at the front page of the paper. There, above the fold, on the right-hand side, was a picture of the writer, his face stretched into a rictus grin. The headline: 'Hemingway Dead of Shotgun Wound; Wife Says He Was Cleaning Weapon'.

Welles took out his cigar, and he rubbed at the spot of flesh between his eyes. There was a trigger of sadness that he did not understand. He read the brief article, reflected on it for a second, and then he read it again. Afterwards, he got to his feet and began to lumber to the kitchen.

Paola came out of the bedroom. 'You knew him, didn't you, Orson?' she asked.

'I did.' Welles took out a large tumbler. He poured some coffee from the steaming pot into a cup, then poured half of that cup into the tumbler. He opened the small freezer and took out the vanilla ice cream and added two scoops of it to the coffee. There was some brandy on the counter, and he topped up the mixture with it, then began to drink. It was a recipe he had come up with at his house

outside Madrid, in the villa where he had been living since once again leaving the US.

Paola looked once more at him. 'Are you OK, Orson?'

'Of course.' He drank from the tumbler, felt the coldness of the ice cream and the dimming heat of the coffee along with the warm kick of the brandy. He held it up. 'The coffee wakes you up,' he said, 'and the brandy keeps you going. The ice cream is good for you.'

Eleven years later, the Spanish writer Ramon Tallista went to Aravaca, on the outskirts of Madrid, to visit Welles at his home. Tallista, who was twenty-three years old and worked for *El País*, would become known later for his complex, florid and elaborate sentences. That day in 1972, however, he had been tasked by his editor with interviewing Welles for a piece following the death of the Russian actor Akim Tamiroff, who had been playing the role of Don Quixote in Welles's forever-stalled adaptation of Cervantes's book.

Tallista arrived early at the villa and was taken through to Welles, who was sitting on the patio. It was late September, and the air was beginning to cool. Welles hauled himself to his feet, his right hand clasped around a cane, when Tallista came on to the patio. He swapped the cane to his left, then shook Tallista's hands. Tallista marked to himself how large and soft Welles's hands were.

The men sat down, and Welles coughed twice. 'Apologies,' he rumbled. 'I have a bad cold that's coming in, and the air here begins to turn damp at this time. I still like to sit out in my garden, though.'

'That's quite all right.' Tallista looked properly at Welles for the first time, and he saw how big the director had become, how he was concurrently so large and rounded but also stiff. He noted that Welles was dressed all in black, and his hair seemed dyed, as if a concession to faded youth, and was slicked back. Welles had some

beard growth, too, and Tallista could see that it was grey. 'Shall we start?'

A chuckle. 'I thought we had. You wanted to know about Akim?'

'I did.'

'He was a delightful actor, and I used him in both *Touch of Evil* and in *Don Quixote*. Well, I *was* using him.' Welles's cheeks shifted slightly downwards. 'We would have done great things together.' Welles looked over at the notepad that Tallista was scratching notes onto. 'Are you writing in Spanish, translating me? Or are you doing it in English, hoping to translate it later on?'

'Spanish. I'm translating you.'

'Very good. Yes, Akim was a great actor. He understood, as all the great directors do – and I would not say I am one of them—' there was that chuckle again '—that it is best not to shoot an actor in colour if they are any good.'

'Why not?'

'Because black and white is always better. That is where the faces play best. You see more of the subtle movements because of the contrast.'

'You said that you are *not* one of the great directors. Most critics would say that you are.'

Welles chuckled again. 'That is because critics are fundamentally unsound! But I will take those compliments anyway, since I am nothing but an old ham.'

'Your recent films...'

'All disasters. *Mr Arkadin* was taken away from me and called *Confidential Report*, and the backers butchered it. It should have been much better. *The Deep*, we will not see in my lifetime. *The Trial*, I hope that people will remember that well.'

'There's also *Chimes at Midnight*.'

Welles nodded, and a pall of seriousness came over his face. 'Nobody saw it, but that's the one that I'd like to be remembered for. If anything, I think that is my favourite of all my pictures.'

'And *Don Quixote*? You've been working on that one for some time.'

'I could have finished it in three weeks if I had had the money, but I didn't. And now Akim has gone on to a better place, I have come to accept that it is over.'

Tallista marked down the notes. Welles reached over and put his hand on his wrist. 'You don't want that reported?' Tallista asked.

Welles chuckled. 'No, just in case. I might meet someone with a sackful of cash that they want to put into it.'

Tallista closed his notebook. 'So, what is next?'

Welles sat back in his chair. 'I have some voiceovers to do, and I'm going to act in a few films. And I'm doing them because I need the money.'

'Surely you have earned enough over the years so that you do not have to work so much any more?'

Welles shook his head. 'A common misconception. No, I am a travelling showman, and I have to go where the work is.'

'But you would like to direct again?'

'I am still directing!' Welles bellowed. He smiled. 'I still have projects, and I'm still putting them together. I will make more pictures before I'm through.'

'Do you like making them? Has it been a life well lived?'

Welles exhaled through his nose, and he thought for a long period. 'I may have done better,' he said, eventually, 'if I had stayed in theatre. I could have done more. Not done it better, mind you, but I could have had a long and fruitful career if I had done that. As it is, I have wasted so much of my life in trying to find funding for

projects that never succeeded or never came into being. And maybe it would have been better if I had stayed within the studio system and made their pictures for them – but then those pictures wouldn't have been mine!'

Tallista opened his notebook and scratched down some more notes. 'You sound like you have made peace with it?'

'I have. And I don't miss Hollywood, although it also has never really missed me. We are alike in that way.'

'You must have fond memories of it.'

'I do. But that is mainly because I was on the inside at the time. The more I look back on it, the worse a place it seems to be. Anyone with any talent was either corrupted or destroyed by that place.'

'Is that why you did not go back last year to get that Oscar? The honorary one?'

Welles nodded. 'John Huston picked it up for me, and he has become a dear friend. I'm going to use him in my next picture.'

'Which is?'

'*The Other Side of the Wind.*'

Tallista looked up. He paused, leaving a gap that Welles could fill. Eventually, he asked, 'What is *The Other Side of the Wind*?'

'It's about a movie director who is very macho. Drinks a lot, shoots guns, is proud of the hair on his chest. The type who goes to bullfights because that is what Ernest Hemingway has taught him to do. That is what our story is about – a man who is like that.'

'He *does* sound like Ernest Hemingway.'

'He does.'

'You knew Hemingway, didn't you?'

'Briefly, shortly, not by much. Our relationship was one that moved so quickly that it barely touched the sides. But I liked him tremendously, and it was always good when we met.'

'And the main character in this film is a movie director, but he's also like Ernest Hemingway? Are you writing about yourself or Ernest Hemingway?'

'Both!' Welles began to stand up. 'Come, walk with me,' he said, leaning on his cane. 'I might need your youth and your strength to get around. I want to show you my garden.'

The two men walked together, Welles hooking his arm into the young man's. The old director guided the pair of them down the steps and onto the path that ran through the garden. He smelled the air, and then he stopped Tallista and tapped his shoulder and looked up.

'Do you smell that? As long as I've been coming to Spain, I've always smelled it. Oranges. They become most pungent at this time of the year when the winter is coming. Or, as much winter as we get down here in Madrid.'

'You like Spain very much?'

'I do. I always have, since I was a boy. Since my first days in Seville, writing pulp fiction and fighting bulls. I don't think life was ever any better after that.'

'And why do you like Spain? What is it about here that brings you back?'

'It is an old-fashioned country, and I am an old-fashioned man. It lives somewhat out of time, as do I. There is not much about the modern world that I do like.'

They began to walk again. Welles walked Tallista down to the end of the swimming pool, where they turned. He walked them along the bottom end of the pool, then turned again. They started to head back towards the patio.

Tallista took out his notebook.

'You want more?' Welles asked, with a chuckle.

'I do.'

'What question do you have?'

'Would you ever make a film about Spain?'

'I have tried, and I would love to.'

'What would that film be about?'

'It'd be an essay, like my most recent one. Cervantes wrote about a man who had gone mad from reading old tales. And he became a knight, and you know he's the most perfect knight there ever was. That was a great world that once existed. It has taken tourism and the modern world to dim that world. I would like to make something about that.'

'What would you call it?'

'*When Are You Going to Finish "Don Quixote"*? That's what people always ask me, so I'll call it that.' Welles laughed, and there was a hoarse rasp behind it. He seemed to be getting tired.

Tallista nodded. The pair of them were walking back up the stairs to the patio. 'I think that's everything,' he said.

'OK.' Welles sounded sad, as if the parting was to make a small cut in him. 'I can give you one last question.'

'How would you like to be remembered?'

'I would like people to say I was good. That's what I want for my children and grandchildren. An idea that I was good. No one writes that in the things they put out about me, but that is what I want. I want them to know that I was good. That would be nice.'

# 14

# A QUIET PLACE IN THE EARTH (1985)

The complicated life of Orson Welles came to an end at some point in the night between 9 and 10 October 1985. He was found at his home in Los Angeles the next morning beside his typewriter. He had been living in the US again since 1974.

There was little surprise at Welles's death. The writer Peter Viertel saw Welles in Paris a few years before, largely trapped in a room at the Hôtel de la Trémoille because of his size and barely able to shuffle to the door to collect his room service orders. And Welles's daughter Christopher Welles thought he had survived ten years longer than he should have.

Welles had appeared the night before his passing on *The Merv Griffin Show*, where he hawked his old memories and told tales of his life in Hollywood and in Europe, everything said with a nod and a wink. He was still large, although he looked thinner and his skin was loose, as if he had lost a great deal of weight in only a short time.

'With me, losing a lot is just a little,' Welles said, laughing, when he came out. He looked tired, his appearance pale and blotchy, and his

hair was thin. There were noticeable liver spots on his forehead. He was suffering, too, from diabetes. Only his voice remained strong.

Welles was in a reflective mood, talking about his former wife Rita Hayworth. 'That's one of the dearest and sweetest women that ever lived,' he said. He spoke sadly about Hayworth's decline from Alzheimer's and of how he had seen a picture of her in a magazine many years before and of how that had first prompted him to meet her. 'We were a long time together,' he reflected. 'I was lucky enough to be with her longer than any of the other men in her life. She is a dear person, and she was a wonderful wife and an extraordinary girl in every way. I've never heard anyone sound like an enemy of hers.'

After the interview had been taped, Welles had gone back to his home at 1717 North Stanley Avenue and passed away while writing up stage instructions for a new project.

A few days after his passing, a funeral was held in a destitute part of downtown Los Angeles, in a funeral home that Christopher Welles remembered as being a like a 'cheap motel room'. There were fewer than a dozen mourners. Paola Mori, his third wife, excluded pretty much everyone from the film industry in Hollywood.

It was a sad, awkward affair that only got worse in the coming months and years. Such was the complexity of Welles's life and of his personal relationships, his funeral was the first time that all three of his daughters had stood together in the same room.

There were other complications. As Christopher Welles observed later: 'Sometime during the night, his heart had stopped. He had died not in Las Vegas, where he maintained a home for the third Mrs Orson Welles, but in Los Angeles, where he had been living openly with his Croatian companion, Oja Kodar.'

Welles and Kodar had met in the early '60s when he was filming *The Trial* in Paris. They had a brief affair, then parted for some years before meeting once again. From there, they remained together for the next two decades. For the whole of this time, he remained married to Paola Mori. It was later claimed that Mori had been unaware of the 'arrangement' until the last year of Welles's life. On the night Welles died, Kodar was visiting family in Europe. After Welles's death, Mori would also exclude her from the funeral.

The two sides began litigation against each other, centring over Welles's estate. In 1982, Welles had written a will that left his Las Vegas home and much of what he owned to Mori, with separate $10,000 bequests for his daughters. The same will left the Los Angeles home and its contents to Kodar. It also contained a proviso that any challenges to it would result in an heir being disinherited.

The following year, 1983, saw Welles and Kodar set up a trust called IDIOM, into which the pair invested $400,000 before his death. And in June 1985, Welles signed over all the rights to his unfinished films to Kodar. A month before he died, Welles signed a promissory note to Kodar for money loaned for the pension scheme of IDIOM. Then, just days before he died, Welles made his Croatian partner – not his wife – a beneficiary for half of his pension plans. The two developments in September and October were not notarised. It was these that Welles's wife Mori challenged in the courts.

But then Mori died in August 1986, as a settlement between the two camps was being reached. In Las Vegas, she was a passenger in a car whose driver pulled out into oncoming traffic and was struck by another vehicle. Mori, the only fatality, died of head injuries. Hers and Welles's youngest daughter, Beatrice, took over as executor of both her parents' estates.

Three months later, the family and Kodar reached an agreement.

Kodar dropped her 50 per cent claim of the pensions. Beatrice, in response, dropped the civil suit initiated by her mother, along with a guarantee that she would not fight for the ownership of the unreleased films. Kodar also picked up the assets of the IDIOM trust, less the $130,000 promissory note.

*The Other Side of the Wind* never appeared in cinemas within Welles's life. Its delay – a book in itself – was due to its funding by the Shah of Iran's brother-in-law, Mehdi Boushehri. After the shah's deposing in 1979, a French court ruled that its ownership belonged to the film company set up by Boushehri, and so for years *The Other Side of the Wind* lay in a French bank vault, unreleased and unreleasable. In fact, it did not appear in a finished state until 2018, thirty-three years after Welles's death, when Netflix used its financial clout to cut through the arguments and issues to finish it and present it to the world.

The ugliness still finished with a beautiful endgame. Beatrice Welles flew to Europe with her parents' ashes in 1987. It was, as Peter Viertel described in his book *Dangerous Friends*, 'a strangely macabre mission for a young woman to undertake while on her honeymoon'.

The ashes of Welles and Mori were placed in separate locations. Mori's remains were taken to Rome and interred there.

But Welles was brought to Spain by his youngest daughter. Beatrice would say later that the decision had been made by her and her mother, citing Welles's love for the south of Spain. They rejected Hollywood, where he had gained his fame, and they rejected, too, his hometown of Kenosha, Wisconsin. Both of them, she said, were places in which her father never felt comfortable.

In May, around eighteen months after his passing, Beatrice placed her father's ashes within an old well on the grounds of the country home of his old friend Ordóñez.

A handful of close friends attended.

Some soil from the bullring was poured on top of the ashes. After so many years, the great director had come home not to where he was born but to where he had chosen to live.

# 'I HAVE MANY STRANGE MEMORIES OF HIM LIKE THAT' (1973)

**W**e arrive back at the beginning.

Welles swung slowly on the chair as he talked. He looked once more at the interviewer. His eyes dulled, as if he were narrating instead what he could see within his mind. 'I saw him in the last year', he said of Hemingway, 'in which he was still entirely in control of himself quite a lot. We never discussed bullfighting, because, except on the subject of Ordóñez, we disagreed profoundly on too many points. And he thought he invented it, you know? He really did think he invented it. Maybe he did.'

He was a great artist, Welles said. The interviewer agreed.

Welles carried on. 'I was enormously fond of him as a man, too, because the thing you never get from his books was his humour. There's hardly a word of humour in a Hemingway book, because he's so tense and solemn and dedicated to what is true and good and all that. But when he relaxed, he was riotously funny. And that was the level that I loved about him, and I enjoyed being with him. I

used to go out and keep him company when he went duck-shooting in Venice in the autumn. I have many strange memories of him like that, and I was enormously fond of him.'

The interviewer pushed a little. 'He was, ultimately,' he said, 'a tragic figure, wasn't he, in that his end was a complete counterpoint to all that he stood for and wrote about?'

Welles tilted his head. A deflection. 'He was sick,' he said, twice. 'But he did talk about suicide. You know that his father killed himself with a gun in the same way? He talked to me about it several times in a sort of obsessive way. But he was a sick man. He was not well mentally. He's not to be judged as himself. The Hemingway we are talking about did not choose his death. He might have, but he wasn't that man.'

When asked if Hemingway had become an old-fashioned writer, Welles shook his head. He said that he thought his old 'friend' had come back into fashion, a little more than ten years after his death. A fallow period followed by one of re-evaluation, then an assured place in the canon.

It was a nice thought, and possibly Welles believed it, too. He may have *wanted* to believe it. Why wouldn't he? It was in 1973 when all his projects were withering on the vine, and *Don Quixote* had been buried, his other films taken from him. *The Other Side of the Wind* was still a distant, unfulfilled dream. Welles probably wanted more. He probably felt that he deserved it, too. He may not have known that he was at the halfway point between Hemingway's death and his own, but it was clear that he was onto the third act of whatever his life story was going to be.

We come to the end of our story. What is left? What of it was true?

Well, truth is often difficult to parse, and it sits often in opposition to fact. Subjective in many instances.

The two men may have been friends, acquaintances and enemies, often all at the same time. They may have been conspirators in a different timeline. What might an Orson Welles-directed version of a Hemingway novel have looked like? What if the recording for *The Spanish Earth* had not resulted in a fistfight? What if they had spent their entire careers intertwined with one another, with Hemingway writing and Welles directing?

Such undertakings could only have been interesting, the meshing point of two of the twentieth century's most prominent cultural figures. They may, together, have been more than they were individually. Or perhaps each would have diminished the other.

It is another question that can be posed but not answered. And maybe that should be the best of it.

After all, there is always some fool that turns up and spoils the fun for everyone else by knowing the correct answer.

# CODA

# TWO BULLS AT REST (2024)

At the beginning of September 2024, as I was putting this book to rest, I took a trip to Ronda, Spain, where Welles is buried. The plan had been to attend the town's Pedro Romero Festival, see a bullfight and pick up some local flavour and colour for A Duel of Bulls: Hemingway and Welles in Love and War.

I had not been in Spain for a few years. The last time I visited was in 2021 when writing my first book, but I was going to Ronda for two reasons: first, to see the part of Spain that both Welles and Hemingway loved most and to see what of it still existed. The second was to have some quiet space where I could work on final edits and emendations. The writing life is such that one can never just take a holiday. My plan, like Hemingway, was to rise early in the morning and work for an hour or two each day before the heat rose too high to make anything else an impossibility. I also took with me my much-thumbed copy of The Face of War by Martha Gellhorn.

The plane from Berlin lifted into the air a minute or two after 6 a.m., banked south and began its course to Málaga.

It was an early morning flight and full apart from the empty seat

beside me, but I could not sleep, so I read some of *The Face of War*, listened to Welles in various interviews and hoped that the journey would not be too onerous.

It was busy when we landed at Málaga, and the airport was throttled with people, some heading into the city or catching coaches further to Marbella or Torremolinos or Estepona. It was hot, the temperature by 10 a.m. having already reached about thirty-two degrees, and there was little shade outside.

There is no direct coach from Málaga Airport to Ronda, and the best you can do is ride half an hour instead into Marbella, coasting along the southern coast of Spain, and from there take another ninety-minute coach ride over the Sierra Blanca mountains and into Ronda.

I waited an hour at Málaga for the next bus and it had been around two hours after my plane had landed once I got off that. The lady selling tickets at the Marbella coach station said that the next bus to Ronda would leave in about five hours' time. I put my luggage into a locker and walked into the centre.

The walk was downhill, much easier than on the way back, and I looked back at the bus station when I was a few hundred feet away to mark in my memory the red-and-white building. It was then that I saw the mountains behind it, and the clouds wrapped around them that looked as dirty as an eiderdown that had been dragged for some distance along a street.

There was not much to the city – Marbella is a stretch of sea next to proliferations of apartment blocks and newly built small white homes, and there were few Spanish locals on its streets. The city had all the appeal of a blank piece of paper. It was mostly the Germans and the British tourists carrying their countries to a new and hotter place.

I eventually made my way back to the bus station and waited two hours in the small cafe for my coach. And then it came and we left quickly, and we seemed to move west at first, past all the apartment blocks and then some more until it was no longer clear when – or, even, if – we had reached the limits of Marbella.

The houses and the apartments became sparser, and the bus began to climb a long and languid route that hugged the side of the mountains. The road was narrow, but the driver seemed so sure of himself that he may only have been a trip or two away from trying it with a blindfold. He drove so tight to the edge that the wheels of the coach skirted continually the cliff that dropped hundreds of feet away. There were no barriers. Few things are as unnerving as a risky bus journey and an overconfident driver.

The bus climbed for about an hour and the cliffs were on our right for some of it, but then they were on our left, and when you looked up, you could see the tops of the mountains and you knew that the dirty-grey cloud must have been all around you. We straightened along that route until we started to come down once again. Now, the land was all dry and dirty scrub, with soil that would break apart under your feet, and the sides of the hills were packed with compact and rough-looking trees.

We began to see Ronda, the back of the town appearing to the left of the coach's window, but the driver did not go straight but looped instead around, circling the town as if it were going to be attacked on its flank. And then there was another climb, and we circled some more corners until a shudder and a halt let us know that we had arrived.

There were to be no bullfights at the Pedro Romero Festival in Ronda that year. At the end of May, the bullring's technical team did

a new inspection of the stone pillars that encircle the structure and pronounced that there were doubts over the safety of the building. A press conference given in June posited that the reason for the declaration was a deterioration in their condition after a rainy winter came on the tail of several years of drought and two summers of extreme heat.

'Consequently,' the leaders of the bullring said in a press conference, calling it a 'postponement', 'we regret to inform you that this year it will not be possible to celebrate the *Goyesca* bullfight or the festivities that accompany it. Security, as you can imagine, is our main concern.'

The main celebrations, however, were set to continue.

In the meantime, they were to work on the building's structural safety.

They said: 'This will aim to ensure many more years of celebrations in this eighteenth-century venue. Like all historical artistic monuments, improvements are a constant that allow the heritage and richness of this unique monument to be preserved.'

My room was at the Hotel Doña Carmen, on Calle Naranja. It was the second time I had stayed there. It was a small and basic place that was half hotel and half hostel. I stayed in the latter part, on the second floor next to a small bathroom. There was a single bed, a wardrobe and a small tight desk. My window overlooked the wall of another building and down onto the roof of the hostel's kitchen. It was a street or two from the town's main bus station, and about a ten-minute walk to the Puente Nuevo, the famous bridge that marks Ronda as a destination for tourists and travellers.

I had first stayed at the Hotel Doña Carmen in 2019, about six months before the world went into lockdown, when I was doing an

earlier trip to follow the vapours and whispers of Orson Welles and Ernest Hemingway.

It felt good to be back, much like slipping into comfortable clothing after the end of a long day or plunging into the company of an old and good friend.

Like Hemingway, I woke early the next morning when it was still cool, and I wrote, working on a magazine article and the manuscript for *A Duel of Bulls*. I started at 6 a.m., right after waking, and then left to swim at 7 a.m. before returning for breakfast at the hotel.

The first morning, I walked down Carrera Espinel towards the historic centre of the town. The street was covered with lines of red, black and white balls strung along lines that shaded the people below. There was a giftshop along there with a weathered statue outside of Don Quixote. Past Don Quixote, I noticed some prints, old photos of Ronda. And in the middle were older photographs of both Hemingway and Welles, taken at different times in the same period.

The photograph of Welles was taken somewhere within the bullring, and he looks hot, his thick and heavy shirt undone to halfway down his chest. His hair is unkempt, there is a cigar in his mouth and he is unshaven. The look on his face is the one of a man in the middle of a great deal of fun. He stands between two nameless bullfighters.

In a different photograph, Hemingway stands next to the same bullfighter but on a different day. The *traje de luces* seems of a different, darker hue. Hemingway, too, appears better dressed for the weather than Welles, in a thin white shirt, a chequered cap on his head. He looks robust, not as thin as he would become, but he looks not old in his face but older. It is the face of experience, albeit one that seems to have picked up a healthy tan.

I took the cards inside and bought them. 'When were these taken?' I asked.

The woman in the shop shook her head. 'I don't know,' she said.

'They look to be from the 1950s?'

'Could be.'

'And the bullfighter?'

She looked down at the postcards. She squinted, began to shake her head again.

'It's the same person in both.'

She looked at me as if I had pointed out that a fish needs water. 'I see,' she said, 'but I don't know who it is. Maybe it is Ordóñez. If Welles and Hemingway were here in Ronda, it is most likely him. Welles was great friends with Ordóñez.'

The bullring was at the end of the Carrera Espinel, close to the bridge. It is the oldest permanent model of its kind in Spain, squat and holding only 6,000 people. The outside walls were white, and the roof was thatched, and inside there were two levels of seating with six or seven rows in each. It was the most basic of rings where even the royal box seemed much more basic than those in Seville or Madrid.

All writers like to talk about what they are writing. 'I'm here to do a book,' I said at the desk, getting a ticket for the self-guided tour. I held up *The Dangerous Summer* and tapped the cover. 'It's about Ernest Hemingway and Orson Welles.'

'Yes, they liked it here,' said the woman, pointing over her shoulder, to the left, at a half-rebuilt restaurant. 'We have a picture of Orson Welles in the cafeteria.'

I stepped over and looked at the picture. It seemed to be taken in the '50s when Welles would have been probably in his late forties,

part of the same set of postcards. He was as big in it as he ever was, and he was unshaven, his hair still black but his beard being mostly grey. He looked to be wearing a dark shirt, probably a deep green although the photograph was in black and white. It looked hot, too, and there was sweat in his hair and a cigar in his mouth.

'Do you have much about him here?'

She seemed to misunderstand the question. 'He was here a lot. He was friends with the Ordóñez family.'

There was little about Welles in the bullring or in the museum that ran along the outer edges of the building. At one point, the tour crossed over the sand of the bullring itself and, unlike Las Ventas in Madrid, you could walk out into the centre and then to the other side.

I stood on the sand, in the heat, and then jumped up and down. The ground was as firm as stone, and there was only a light dusting of sand on its top. Somewhere, near where the bulls came out, the guide said, was where Ordóñez had his ashes placed after his death.

There was no Hemingway, either, until you walked into the gift-shop on the way out, and there were copies of *The Sun Also Rises* and *Death in the Afternoon*. My copy of *The Dangerous Summer* was the only one that day in the bullring.

Lunch was at the Restaurante Pedro Romero, where I ate cold garlic soup, then rabbit cooked also in garlic. When the soup came, it was delicious and served with bread. It felt both enormously wrong and satisfying to crumble and rip at it above the soup, showering bread-crumbs into the plate.

The silver-haired waiter, who was of average height and lean, with a stoop, had put me in a room at the back by myself. He wore black trousers, with a black polo shirt with the red emblem of the restaurant stitched into it.

The walls of the backroom were covered with photographs and painted posters of bullfighting. There was a cape in a frame on the wall that had once belonged, it said, to the famed *torero* Manolete.

The waiter came by halfway through to ask if the food was OK.

'Splendid. Thank you.'

'Good.'

'May I ask a question?'

He nodded. 'My English…' He trailed off. 'But I try.'

I gave him my usual spiel. 'I'm here to write a book,' I said. 'It's about Orson Welles and Ernest Hemingway.' I held up again *The Dangerous Summer*.

'They came here a lot.'

'I see. Did they come here?'

'No. This restaurant – 1974. He came to the bullring but not to here. But he was a friend of Ordóñez.'

Afterwards, I walked down through the Paseo de Blas Infante, a small park that marks the border of the town of Ronda and the spectacular gorge. There were at its entrance two six-foot-tall sculptures, one adorned with the face of Hemingway and the other with the face of Welles. They faced each other and the stones were the colour of Spanish sand.

The inscription for Hemingway read: *He wrote simply, with a limited repertoire, and his work was simple, classical and tragic.*

For Welles, the sculptor had used Welles's famous quote about a man being from the place where he chooses to die, adding: *Ronda was chosen; he wanted to be a citizen of Ronda for ever. His ashes were deposited here in El Recreo de San Cayetano, for eternity.*

I went down through the park, past the men and women selling trinkets, and went to the low stone wall that overlooked the gorge,

and I breathed in the heavy, dry air. Night was beginning to come, the shadows seeming to grow from the wall, spreading their way across the stone. The sky was pink and it was grey, and the temperature had moved to a comfortable level. The world seemed to be quieting piece by piece.

There was a stage at the bottom of the park that overlooked the El Tajo Gorge, where five or six flamenco dancers were practising for a show. They moved and they shook their figures in one direction, then another, and their long dresses in many different colours swayed with them as they practised their moves, going one way and then another. There were the loud *clock* sounds of their feet hitting the stone floor, and behind them, the sun had broken through the clouds for the final time that day.

They looked something akin to angels.

I circled through the park and went back into the main part of the town, then crossed Ronda's famous bridge, the Puente Nuevo, and walked for a few minutes into the town's Moorish side. Flocks of birds flew under the bridge and stopped here and there to rest in the cliffs, before going out once more into the air. I watched the crows glide, then wrap their wings around themselves and dive thirty or so feet to build velocity, then spread those wings again to catch the air and take them back up. Dive, rise, glide, dive, rise, glide.

The city felt much different than Marbella. Smaller, more modest. There was an attitude of take or leave it, which translated into a sense of civic pride. If it felt more like the undiluted Spain than anyone else, it may have been because it felt like nowhere else in Spain.

I wanted, on my second day in Ronda, to travel the three or four

miles outside of the town to visit where Welles was buried in 1985 – the ranch belonging to the Ordóñez family. I wanted to pay some sort of vexatious tribute after nearly a year of writing this book.

I had sent a recorded letter a few months before but received no reply. So when I was in Ronda, I phoned the farm early one morning with a number I had found on the internet. Someone answered and quickly said, '*No Ingles*,' and then they were gone.

I tried, anyway, to go. It was my last day in Ronda and the temperature was high. There was no public transport there and I thought of taking a taxi, but the ranch was in the middle of nowhere and, in the midday heat, I did not want to hike back, uphill, for over an hour.

So I did not go. I went back into the historic centre of Ronda and I walked halfway down into the gorge so I could look up at, instead of down from, the Puente Nuevo. And that was that. It was time to go. I realised that going to where Welles was buried might have been an incursion. What more was needed? His life had ended in Los Angeles and his life's story ended in the valleys of southern Spain, amongst friends and in a land that he had loved. It was right for someone to have that measure of peace.

I had decided, like many do and on the recommendation of the writer Brin-Jonathan Butler, to climb down into the gorge beneath the famous bridge. To get there, I crossed over the bridge from the new part of the town into the Moorish quarter, then through a gate in the city wall and down some paths that swung abruptly three or four times to a lookout point a few hundred metres below.

The view was magnificent, but I decided to go deeper, and I gave up the path most taken in order to walk down through the trees and the vines.

I went first along the ridge to where a tunnel went into the side of

the cliff. That was carved deep into a rock, but it smelled of things too natural and so I turned, then headed downhill and into the trees where a disused building stood, its roof open to the Andalucian sky. Roots and branches had come into the building and the floor was littered with rubble and all the windows were gone, so I passed through briefly and came to its edge where a stone wall ran beneath it by a few feet and at an angle. I jumped, landed, then climbed down from the stone wall and went further into the trees, scrabbling down a steep hill to another path that I followed out.

The heat was intense, and the shade from the trees offered little, but I stayed as much as I could beneath the trees; it was supposed to nudge forty degrees that day, and I drank liberally from my water bottle and carried on in the heat until I came to a path, this one a few hundred feet beneath the lookout point.

I was exposed now and so I continued to go down to the hostel in the valley, and I ate lunch there with glasses of water, rocks of ice in them as big as a child's fist, and I sat in the little shade and looked up at the bridge, some 600 feet above me.

It was a remarkable sight. An engineering marvel. Generations had built it, one after the other, boys becoming men then fathers then grandfathers, dying before its completion. And still it stood over the gorge.

It was the last night, and I went off Carrera Espinel and spent an hour or so at Los Cristales in Plaza del Socorro. It was a small place run by family. Most of the tables were outside.

I ate cheese and bread, with marmalade, and I sat next to a table of middle-aged Spaniards, talking about things I would never know in ways that I would never understand. They were smoking and vaping, talking as the night went deeper into darkness. There were

many beer bottles and wine glasses on their table, and they were doing nothing other than enjoying themselves and each other.

If there had been an almost-perfect place to stop, that might have been it. But there had been another moment earlier that night, with Paco Seco.

Seco was a guitar player who lived in Ronda. He played concerts for small crowds most nights. That evening, I arrived a few minutes before he was supposed to start, and he shrugged, and he said, 'No concert tonight. I'm not playing for only one or two. But the coach parties will come into Ronda tomorrow and there will be many then.' He smiled. 'I'm sorry.'

'Would you be so kind', I asked, 'to play a little for me?'

'Of course,' he said, picking up the guitar next to him. He started to play, and his fingers began to run up and down the guitar, and the sweetest music began to fill the room. It was just the two of us. I picked up a plastic chair and put it down in front of him. He nodded his head at the sheets of music on the stand. 'I like to practise with new stuff; it helps me keep the fingers fresh.'

He played with his eyes closed, his head tilting this way and then that. It is hard to appreciate what you do not understand, but it looked as if he was dreaming of something. Sometimes, he moved his head closer to the body of the guitar and cocked his ear as if he were listening for something else beyond the music. Maybe he was. Maybe it was all part of the performance.

And maybe that was the end, this private concert in Ronda between two men, a guitar player and a guy who had made the decision to write a book about two other men enjoying life. One searching for the moment, another one just enjoying it. And maybe that was the whole point – to just accept that the most important thing after all was to be in the moment.

CODA

Maybe that was it. Maybe that was the secret to all of it. Maybe that was the secret to everything.

Maybe that was the only thing.

# NOTES ON *A DUEL OF BULLS*

**I** wrote at the start of this book that it was never meant to be a serious academic work. There is a lot in this book that has been changed or simplified to make the narrative flow more smoothly. The aim in all of it was not to obscure or change the truth of the facts but to grease them for a better narrative. I am a storyteller and not an academic.

However, all of *A Duel of Bulls* is based on fact.

One of the most notable changes is the date on which Welles and Houseman broadcast their version on the radio of *A Farewell to Arms*, with Katharine Hepburn. While the book was indeed adapted for a one-hour radio show with *The Campbell Playhouse*, the actual date it was transmitted was in 1938, not a year later as *A Duel of Bulls* makes out. The reason for this is simple – that chapter was about the fragmentation of Welles's and Houseman's friendship, so it made sense in the context of *A Duel of Bulls* that it should take place against the backdrop of a Hemingway adaptation.

There are many, many great books, documentaries and academic papers on Welles and Hemingway. I encourage you, if you are serious about learning about their lives, to read them.

Regarding Hemingway, I highly recommend the five-volume series on his life by Michael Reynolds, along with the biographies by Mary Dearborn and A. E. Hotchner. The three-part PBS documentary by Ken Burns is also a remarkable piece of work. I also highly recommend the *Ernest Hemingway: Selected Letters*, edited by Carlos Baker.

For Hemingway's later life, I also read *Autumn in Venice* by Andrea di Robilant and *Running with the Bulls* by Valerie Hemingway. *Autumn in Venice* deals with his visit to Venice in 1948 and his relationship with Adriana Ivancich, an entanglement that in 2025 we would have no compunction about calling inappropriate. The relationship between the two has been written about widely over the years, in various biographies, but the best book about the pair is undoubtedly *Autumn in Venice*.

The best biographies on Welles are, no doubt, the three-part series by the great actor Simon Callow (*Orson Welles: The Road to Xanadu*; *Hello, Americans*; *One-Man Band*) and *Young Orson* by Patrick McGilligan. The best screen portrayal of the Destitute King is that of Christian McKay in *Me and Orson Welles*. I can also recommend the documentaries *Magician: The Astonishing Life and Work of Orson Welles*, *This Is Orson Welles* and the BBC's two-part *Arena* series.

The documenting of Welles's life has mostly focused on his early years. His later years were described well in *This Is Orson Welles* by Peter Bogdanovich and *In My Father's Shadow* by Christopher Welles.

Other works that were of great use were *The View from the Ground* and *The Face of War* by Martha Gellhorn, along with Caroline Moorehead's Gellhorn biography. I very much liked Antony

Beevor's *The Battle for Spain* along with Amanda Vaill's *Hotel Flori-da* for their portrayals of the Spanish Civil War.

There were many more sources used for *A Duel of Bulls*. I have linked to them on my website – www.petecarvill.com.

I suspect there will be controversy over my adjustments to the fabric of history when writing *A Duel of Bulls*. People will say that this thing or that thing is too important or not important enough, that a book that is essentially non-fiction should contain no fiction-al elements. That in making changes, one disrespects the subject.

All of it is academic. But every work of fact is a work of fiction. Storyteller here, not historian.

Besides, to paraphrase Marlene Dietrich at the end of *Touch of Evil*: 'They were some kind of men. What does it matter what you say about people?'

# THE PEOPLE IN
## *A DUEL OF BULLS*

**B**oth men were peripatetic in their lives and, consequently, their friendships had a habit of ebbing and waning, which means that some people appear heavily in *A Duel of Bulls* but subsequently disappear. Their presences within the book are short and sweet and hopefully they are missed afterwards – but that, after all, is life.

MARY WELSH HEMINGWAY outlived her husband by over two decades and continued to reside in their Idaho home. She died in New York but is buried in Ketchum alongside her husband.

JOHN 'BUMBY' HEMINGWAY died in 2000. Since his death, stories have emerged about relations within his own family. It seems that Greg 'Gig' Hemingway may not have been the darkest character with the Hemingway name.

GREG 'GIG' HEMINGWAY, meanwhile, suffered from acute gender dysphoria, eventually transitioning in 1994, taking the name

Gloria. Still suffering, Gig oscillated between the two names and identities up until death, in a Miami prison cell, in 2001. Hopefully, Gig is now at peace.

VALERIE HEMINGWAY, Gig's wife, is still alive and – yes – she was indeed the young Irish woman named Valerie who served as Hemingway's secretary in the early '60s. She met Gig after Hemingway's death, and the pair married and had a family.

PATRICK HEMINGWAY, at the time of writing, is still alive.

MARTHA GELLHORN survived Ernest Hemingway and went on to become the world's greatest war reporter, before dying in 1998.

PAULINE HEMINGWAY died in 1951, aged fifty-six, as is outlined in *A Duel of Bulls*.

HADLEY RICHARDSON passed away in 1979, aged eighty-seven.

ADRIANA IVANCICH went on to marry and have two sons. She died in 1983. Her relationship with Hemingway has been open to debate in the years since and will probably remain that way as long as books are debated. She was survived by her husband and two sons.

SIDNEY FRANKLIN died penniless in New York in 1976, largely forgotten.

JOHN DOS PASSOS died, celebrated but lacking Hemingway's cultural force, in 1970. Their relationship never recovered after

Spain, nor did the circumstances of José Robles's fate ever become clear.

The German photographer GERDA TARO was killed in Spain in 1937 in an accident, the details of which are still unclear, even so many years after her passing. The most accepted explanation is that she was standing on the running boards of a truck, which was run into by a tank. For unclear and unknown reasons, she is buried in Paris in Père Lachaise Cemetery, not far from the grave of Édith Piaf.

Taro's companion ROBERT CAPA was originally named 'André Friedmann'. He and Taro worked together under the adopted name of 'Robert Capa'. After her death, he took on the name as his own. He died in 1954 in Vietnam after stepping onto a landmine while working. His book *Slightly Out of Focus* is tremendous.

The 'commie reporter' S. B., who cannot be named due to legal reasons, is a reference to Jean Ross, a dedicated communist, war reporter, former actress and dancer, and the inspiration for Christopher Isherwood's most famous character from *Goodbye to Berlin*. Versions of Jean Ross have been played over the decades by Julie Harris, Imogen Poots and – most famously – Liza Minnelli.

JOHN HOUSEMAN died in 1988. By the 1950s, as is alluded to in *A Duel of Bulls*, he and Welles had gone through a bitter falling-out. One of my favourite stories about Houseman, which is not in the book, is that in the late 1970s he took the actor Christopher Reeve to one side and said, 'It's very important that you become a serious classical actor. Unless they offer you a shitload of money to do

something else.' Reeve, who had become the lead in the *Superman* films, often told this story on late-night talk shows.

MARC BLITZSTEIN, the musician who initially linked Welles and Hemingway, died in 1964, murdered in Martinique by three sailors he had picked up in a bar.

Of Welles's family, his daughters CHRISTOPHER and BEATRICE, from his marriage to Virginia Nicolson and Paola Mori, are still alive. His middle daughter, REBECCA, died in 2004. Despite his longing for a male heir, Orson Welles never knew of a secret grandson born in 1966 to Rebecca, who was given up for adoption and who himself died in 2010. The truth of that story, gleaned through the documentary *Prodigal Sons*, is indeed stranger than fiction.

Orson Welles is also rumoured to have fathered two other sons, although the truth of that matter remains rightfully murky. One of them, as alluded to in *A Duel of Bulls*, is thought to be the film director Michael Lindsay-Hogg, son of Geraldine Fitzgerald. According to Lindsay-Hogg, blood tests regarding his parentage have been inconclusive. Some have also disputed the timing of his conception, saying that Welles and Fitzgerald were not together whenever it could have happened. The second son that Welles is believed to have fathered was with the actress and TV personality Vampira, although that tale stretches credulity.

VIRGINIA NICOLSON, the first wife of Orson Welles, died in 1996.

RITA HAYWORTH died in 1987. She suffered with undiagnosed Alzheimer's for many years. Initially thought to be the result of alcoholism, her condition was only properly diagnosed later in life.

PAOLA MORI, as described in *A Duel of Bulls*, died in 1986. The Welles estate is managed by Beatrice Welles at the time of writing, who is a staunch advocate for animal rights.

OJA KODAR, at the time of writing, is still alive. She fiercely protects the legacy and work of Orson Welles.

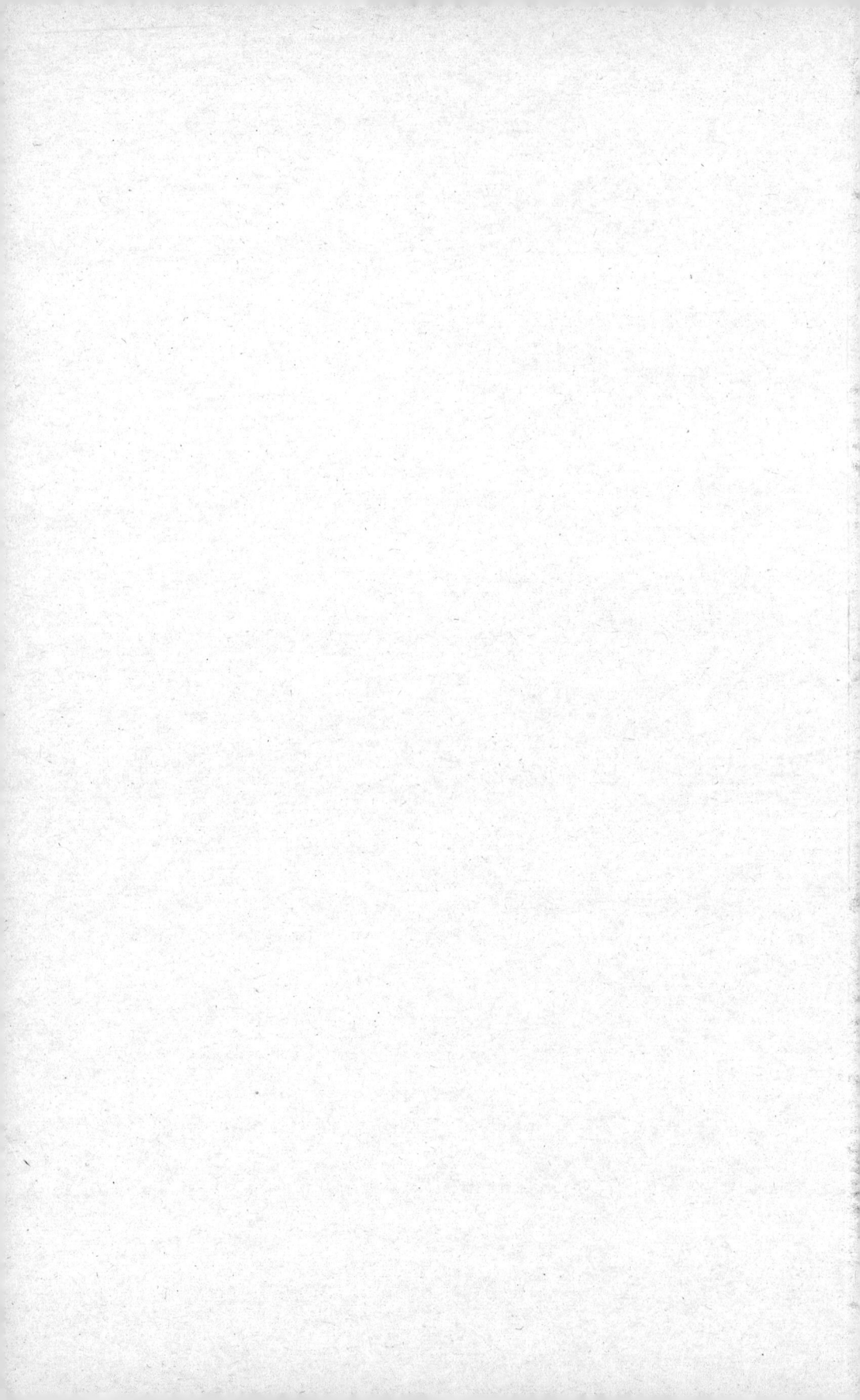

"Orson Welles's and Ernest Hemingway's histrionic lives both occupied the twentieth century like Moby Dick in a goldfish bowl. Finally, here is a book that offers the rare amusement and pleasure of how their mythic paths crossed on the world's stage. There are fine moments from Pete Carvill's *A Duel of Bulls* that feel like little treasures from an unpublished chapter of *A Moveable Feast* that finally found their way to the page."

"In this ambitious, beautifully written book, Pete Carvill playfully and exactingly explores not only the never-before-examined relationship between two of the most influential artists of the twentieth century but also the interplay and nature of self-myth versus truth in art and in all of our lives. *A Duel of Bulls* is a marvellous book I wish I'd written and one I will not only reread time and again but will damn well purchase as presents for friends."

"An evocative and atmospheric book, full of imagination and empathy for the men at its heart and the connections between them. From its conception to its execution, it tells a powerful tale about people and the stories they tell – the stories of others and of themselves."